Don't Call Me Doc

Tales of a football medic in a league of his own

Simon Leeson

Anything can be achieved in small, deliberate steps. But there are times you need the courage to take a great leap; you can't cross a chasm in two small jumps.
David Lloyd George

I feel love...
Donna Summer

David Lloyd George was a Prime Minister and native of North Wales whilst Donna Summer was neither of those things: yet both described the essential ingredients of our ambitious extended family that is Bangor 1876.

Football is a game that forms communities, kinship and makes the impossible possible. Comedy moments are plentiful. The TV pundit and former footballer Chris Kamara missing a sending off whilst he was reporting on-air for Sky Sport in 2011 was a classic. The dreaded score predicted by Eric Morecombe finally happened some years later after a penalty shoot-out in the Scottish League Cup in 2018: producing the commentator's nightmare score line of East Fife four, Forfar five. Football clichés tickle me: footballers reflect by being rueful of their errors and seem to spend time ruing when they have time to rue. I suspect that they have time to do other things occasionally, and in fairness, they may be capable of other emotions. And for that skilful or perhaps lucky manager in charge of a club for a decade, being described by sports reporters as providing a ten-year tenure. These are all attractions that could draw the fan close into the personalities of the game. The smaller the club, the closer you can get. I didn't have any interest in lower league football, that is until I received a message one day.

The following account is of my experience as a medic confronting a whole world of new experiences and meeting people who have made my life so much more rewarding than I could have anticipated. Largely for quite unexpected reasons.

This is my world

I couldn't think of a more idyllic place to be on a sunny, warm Saturday afternoon in late March. The winter rains had done their worst in the preceding months and had now gone away. The thick grey curtains of clouds which seemed to be permanent residents in North Wales had parted company on this day to reveal a bright blue yonder. I was in Llanberis, a small former slate mining town nuzzling at the base of Snowdon, the highest mountain in Wales and looking austere yet protective high above. The main street was lined with small tea shops, cafés and pubs, ideal to welcome any visitor whether a walker, climber or a football tourist like me. No one is in a hurry and people were laughing, sharing a beer or planning their day ahead. Except me.

After researching in advance where I could park my car and make a dash for the football ground, the pay and display machine didn't work. The awkward little jobsworth wouldn't except my cash nor my card. I pressed the button for English rather than Welsh for my payment instructions but then the machine lost interest in me. My remonstrations to the hunk of metal came to nought. Do I take a chance to dump the car and not pay? Are the park wardens here in Llanberis really mean as they are outside my gym back home? After some thought, and a bit of impatient pacing around the entirely indifferent ticket machine, I decided to move the car to a free spot in a side street but much further from the ground. Now I was in a rush. I found the ground wedged in the middle of town conveniently close to a pub and some cake shops. Too late to indulge. However, the entrance to the ground remained well camouflaged from the occasional predatory away fan. There were rather a lot of them on this day as Llanberis were playing Bangor 1876. My team. Following an almost complete circumnavigation of the ground I spotted the entrance. I thought I would play the age card when I had to fork out for my entry ticket. When I asked for a retired concession I got a suspicious look from a stern looking bloke collecting admission fees. He looked me up and down.

"How old are you?"

I instantly took that as a complement.

"60."

"Full price then."

I guessed my David Cassidy good looks hadn't deserted me entirely but I suspect the real reason I had to pay full price was just for my cheek as an opposition supporter. I had to root around in the depths of my pockets to dig out four pounds for the entry ticket. Damn. I suppose that made up for not paying for parking. At least it was cheaper than a Premier League game, by some margin.

I ended up going to Llanberis alone as all of my usual crowd was otherwise occupied that Saturday. I couldn't pass on an afternoon visit to such a beautiful place. The unseasonable breakthrough of spring sunshine was a pleasant change to the previous lingering dregs of winter gloom albeit in the notoriously fickle microclimate of the locality. Still wise to bring a coat. There was a gentle breeze on my face, I was watching a football game and our lads were putting up a good show in an away game against the unmistakable backdrop of the mountains of Snowdonia and behind me was Lake Padarn with the sunlight flickering from its undulating surface like clouds of evening fireflies. Clear cool air almost tasted sweet with a barely perceptible scent of early blossom. Above were pastel shades of sky blue mixed with occasional half-hearted white clouds, dropping onto a nutmeg brown of the jutting mountains still clinging to the last of their winter snowcaps and a deep green of the pine forests and fields of the lower slopes providing the breath-taking amphitheatre to showcase

2

scurrying actors in a play: the deep blues of Bangor 1876 and the yellows of Llanberis. As the play progressed I figured my Saturday just couldn't get any better as I bathed in the early spring sunshine in such a beautiful location. But it could, and it was time to stop dreaming and focus on the important action.

We might be in North Wales but this is football. Rugby Union may be loved by some but football is a big deal in North Wales. Corrig McGonigle, our diminutive striker was through on goal and with a touch of angels wafted the ball over the approaching helpless oppo goalie into an empty net. 0-1! But beware. In our league in Wales, each team supplies a linesman and it just happened that their linesman was covering Corrig's sensational dart forward to bamboozle the Llanberis defensive line. Despite what seemed to me as an obvious conflict of interest, the linesman decided it was in his gift to flag offside. His opinion was not universally shared. Insurrection threatened as the kindly folk supporting Bangor 1876 suggested that the decision made by the deluded linesman may have had something to do with him being part of the Llanberis team. This was reasonably politely rebuffed. Sadly, in the absence of the video assistant referee, usually abbreviated to VAR, or any fourth official that was the end of it. No goal.

The second half proceeded much the same way with our lads dictating the play, the sun in my face and all that, but there were still no goals. We really needed the win! With 15 minutes to go, the right back for Llanberis pulled up with an injury and had to be substituted. That was quite good for us as he was good for them. Within a minute, Corrig was scythed down by their goalie without mercy or apparent concern for the consequence inside the Llanberis box. But before a penalty could be considered the ball broke to our left where their injured right back should have been and our striker Jamie 'Pets' Petrie smashed the loose ball into the back of the net. Cue flare as blue smoke billows from our end of the pitch acting as a safety valve releasing the growing tension from the 1876 faithful. No offside as their linesman was at the other end of the pitch and so we had a just decision from our very own linesman and my restful idyll was restored. I had the sun on my face and life was good.

Jonathan Ervine, our wisecrack press reporter headlined his subsequent weblog match report as 'Pet rescue'. Indeed, it was.

My introduction to 1876

One day, whilst I was doing nothing in particular, I had a WhatsApp message from my mate Glynne.

"Do you want to be the football team medic?"

I thought for approximately six nanoseconds.

"You bet!"

My life has not been the same since.

It was early summer in 2021 and I had retired from working as a consultant gynaecologist in the NHS two months before. I planned to work part-time in medicine in my old post and do some voluntary work but the voluntary work had not happened as then we were 18 months into the Coronavirus pandemic. Opportunities for voluntary work had evaporated. Unexpectedly I had time on my hands.

The club in question was Bangor 1876 and my mate just happened to be its chairman. I had not heard of Bangor 1876, although I was aware of the neighbouring club Bangor City. It was pre-season for CPD Bangor 1876 after being champions of the North Wales Coast West Football League Division One, winning all 16 league games. That was their first, and only season, in competitive football after being formed and was concluded early during the outset of the pandemic. There was no football for the following year for the same reason. As the pandemic had lost a complete season for amateur football, Bangor 1876 found themselves a division lower than where they intended to find themselves in what should have been their third season in business. Their focus was to develop a core of staff suitable for promotion into the higher tiers of Welsh amateur football.

I must confess right now that I am not Welsh but an Essex boy and my family are from the North of England.

However, I moved to Manchester at the age of three and so have little recall of the beautiful rural Essex flatlands, the farmers' fields and small towns where my family lived, south of Cambridge except for the brief time I was stuck in Addenbrooke's Hospital in Cambridge after breaking my leg. It was a foolish injury after tripping over wire in a fence whilst losing control of my trike. I was two and my only experience of sports injury if you can call it that. I remember getting a huge lollipop as compensation from my no doubt anxious parents, I suspect to keep me quiet whilst manfully controlling my emotions in dealing with the excruciating pain of a broken limb. Moving to Manchester meant I never quite acquired the Manc twang but was indoctrinated to follow the only worthy football outfit in town, that of the light blue variety at a time when we truly shone with the likes of Franny Lee, Mike 'buzzer' Summerbee and Nijinsky himself, my favourite of all, the king, Colin Bell. That was a time, I guess like now, when Manchester City actually won stuff. When I was a boy I had a picture of King Col staring down at me from my bedroom wall, inspiring me to be heroic and truly great. He was a modest man with nothing to be modest about. These demigods knew all about having a good time which invariably involved collecting trophies but also having a punch up at some time before the final whistle. So, I thought football was fun, though I had no ability to take up the game personally. Then came the dark times of relegation after relegation but sometimes there were high points as if almost by accident. The 3-0 drubbing of AC Milan was a game to behold and that game against Gillingham at Wembley after winning a penalty shoot-out and promotion from the third tier of English league football left the blue half of Manchester needing oxygen.

My work took me to North Wales 25 years ago. I remember reading the job advert. I was in the middle of a busy gynaecology clinic in a large Mancunian Victorian workhouse style old fashioned hospital and enduring the daily grind of gridlock traffic queues, black stone buildings and streets without trees. The years of industrial pollution had snuffed out countless generations of life before their time around there and had painted the landscape with a featureless charcoal grey from which I ached to escape. But Wales, a country that enjoys singing, poetry and Rugby Union as national pastimes and where football is at best a second thought, a country where there are 10 million sheep outnumbering Welsh people by more than three to one, somehow didn't seem a natural fit. That changed following a drive from my subsequent posting in Preston, taking me past endless fields and mountains and along the beautiful North Walean coastline. The pre-interview grovel with my prospective consultant colleagues in Bangor was a joy. They seemed to like me. Even better, there was countryside wherever I looked and the hospital in question at Bangor was a modern looking hospital called Ysbyty Gwynedd which was perched on a hill from where there were views of Anglesey and Snowdonia. That was the job for me and I was fortunate enough to get it. My colleagues were great too! Ysbyty Gwynedd was the model hospital with perfect government performance statistics in the hit TV series *Yes Minister* because in that TV show it was brand new in the 1980s, and was yet to have any patients! Its performance hasn't been so good in real life since then as it has had patients. Lots of them. And I've been working there too. Also, I found out that Ysbyty Gwynedd was built on a previous gypsy site and the land was supposed to be haunted. That put me off being in late at night. But less of that.

Now I am a convert to the glorious way of life in North Wales: I love the people, the lack of traffic and the bewilderingly beautiful hills and sea. I had to commute a little more to see my football team in Manchester and eventually other commitments meant that I saw less and less live action. Anyhow, football got me into enough trouble with my family, whom I care about dearly, and occasionally, for some reason, people I have never met before. I just couldn't understand why. Time for a change of focus. Bangor 1876 seemed to be just the thing for me.

A gynaecologist for a male-only team medic?

On the football pitch, as in my day job, my medical skills have been put to the test. There are no clinics, no patients in their beds for me to review, no operations and no colleagues for me to advise and educate about the brilliance of my craft. I must admit I did not have it all my own way when I worked in a hospital as a consultant. Before retirement, I had looked after women with all sorts of complicated problems, and yet, after 35 years in my trade I must admit that I am no nearer to understanding the superior species than I was as a timid teenager. They are truly an otherworldly creation. They can multitask: be mothers, have several jobs, be carers and indeed, the list goes on and on. They can be right before there is even a question to be right about. The men's first team at Bangor 1876 however is a different beast entirely. A plain speaking, unassuming, flatulent, verbally diverse group of young men who have one thing in common. Football.

So what core skills can an experienced obstetrician and gynaecologist bring to the table for our players? Very approximately nothing. None need smears, a forceps delivery or a hysterectomy pitch side. None, as yet, have asked for hormone replacement therapy nor advice about their sex lives. I am thankful for that at least. Players are even reluctant to get injured seeing me in the dugout. I was certainly taken from my comfort zone. However, YouTube gives sound instruction in recommending ice packs, elevation and strapping for virtually everything except nose bleeds. It seems you can learn all matters about everything from YouTube from wiring a plug to landing a plane. As long as I remember to skip the ads and not watch those by mistake. Even I may be able to learn about soft tissue injuries to get me through the season, with considerable additional help from my physio colleagues at Bangor 1876, Rhys and Trudy. They continuously, and patiently, advise me when I go wrong. I learnt an acronym PRICE, that is protect from further injury, rest the affected area, ice for 20 minutes, compress and elevate. Oh, and allow for appropriate recovery time. Sounds straightforward but that was only a start. Little by little, I was able to deal with the nuances of caring for injuries apart from massage which sadly remains beyond my modest physiotherapy skills. I must admit I am used to dealing with high pressure situations, which I think helps me to keep players on that football pitch for as long as is reasonable and to remove them even if they feel otherwise. A sponge and cold water can only do so much.

Most people have slightly odd dreams and I am no different. A recurring dream I have is a perfectly reasonable scenario of turning up at work with no clothes and then wondering how I rescue the situation. That somewhat cold and pink vulnerability is a similar feeling I experience at Bangor 1876 waiting for the next medical flashpoint. Head injuries and lacerations are fine. That brings me back to my days working in the Emergency Department in Salford as a junior doctor. You never knew what you would see next. For instance, there was a joiner who tried to get into a cubicle to see me but he couldn't. That was because he had managed to put a nail through his finger with a nail gun. Unfortunately, he turned up with an eight-foot piece of wood that he nailed himself to. Another turned up without his thumb. I cannot remember how it fell off but the problem was that it wasn't there and it wasn't hidden in the patient's clothing despite a careful search. Somehow, we established that it was somewhere on Eccles Old Road requiring the services of our friends from the local constabulary who were regular helpers in Salford Royal casualty. The missing finger was retrieved from a gutter and reunited with its owner. Surgically. I am not sure how well the thumb and the remainder of the man fared in the longer term but it was, at least initially, a happy reunion. Then there was the Indian lady who spoke no English who was clearly about to have a baby. She was on a hospital trolley and writhing about in pain. By that time, I was specialising in obstetrics and gynaecology. She was in a maternity unit. So far, so good. Except that there was only her and I in a lift which had broken down between floors and she required an emergency Caesarean section. A situation solved by manhandling the lift doors and a lot of screaming. From both of us. All these problems and many, many more were my bread and butter. A whinging footballer rolling over several times in the mud only to recover to 100% normality in seconds seemed far more tricky to me. I needed to pick up the behavioural nuances of the team and sense when they were hurt and in trouble. These seemed more motherly than medical skills.

The next thing I needed was a bag. The medical man always has a bag. I needed to fill it with stuff. A sponge and some water. And I guess some other bits. That meant speaking to Rhys and Dafydd.

Rhys and Dafydd

Rhys Last introduced himself on his first day at the club by reminding me that I delivered him as a baby 24 years before. A detail I had forgotten but it was nice to be up to speed with that one. With a twist of serendipity Rhys is a keen sportsman, loves his rugby and is a physiotherapist. Clearly this was very useful for me as I realised that I wasn't any good at physiotherapy. He gave me several lessons in managing key injuries. Importantly Rhys had to give me his list for bits of kit which needed replacing and I would contact Dafydd Hughes in his esteemed role as our Club Secretary, supplies man and photographer, to get them. He is a retired town planner and his methodological approach to everything is a considerable asset. Quite why I had to be part of the bureaucratic process was unclear to me but having just completed a life sentence in the NHS, bureaucracy was part of my DNA.

Dafydd turns out to be the fastest delivery man in world history. I can send an email asking for bandages and whatnot to be supplied by Dafydd, without fail, into the stockroom at our ground called Treborth within a few days. Guaranteed. The slowest part of the delivery pathway is the speed at which my email can arrive at Dafydd's computer. Dafydd is as fastidious with details as he is fast and the complete order is delivered in full every time. Into the locked stockroom cupboard. So, all I needed to get into the stockroom cupboard was a key, and then I could be a pretend physio. This turned out to be a work in progress for the remainder of the season.

I must stress that Rhys is not our only physiotherapist but works in partnership with Trudy, both of whom have taught me, with great patience, the basics of assessing and managing soft tissue injuries. Although Trudy helped me in the early part of the season, and indeed was the only physio before Rhys arrived, she was unable to attend most of the games in the latter half. As it happened, thankfully, Trudy was able to return as normal the following summer. Overall, it worked out that the two of them managed to cover almost all games, usually leaving me to manage the more serious injuries such as head injuries and broken limbs. Thankfully these don't happen too often which gives me plenty of time to watch the football. In my wisdom, I thought I should order a collapsible stretcher. The stretcher promptly disappeared. It is not missed. I contrived to order for me the biggest physio bag I have ever seen. Neither Rhys nor Trudy wanted such a large bag but it would do the job nicely for me.

My kit bag and I. A match made in heaven. A modelling contract is anticipated.

By the time I stuffed everything in I thought I needed for a game, my bag looked as if I was going on holiday for a week in the sun. On the plus side I can gorge on all the supplies in the stockroom before Rhys and Trudy get to them. Whenever I can get the cupboard key. Then I return to the pitch side or the dressing room to see Rhys or Trudy, I hand out what they need as if I have ordered these trinkets myself and I then take all the plaudits. I have no magic sponge but there is pretty well everything else. I have bandages, tapes, Deep Freeze, Deep Heat, painkillers and even stuff for an emergency mini-tracheostomy for airway obstruction which I hope I never have to use. I have nicked my massage gun from home that I used for a hamstring injury I suffered seemingly throughout lockdown. I also figured I needed some Epipens to treat any anaphylactic reactions due to any sudden severe allergy. This required a bit of investigative work to see how I could obtain a private prescription as there seemed to be none going spare for me to 'borrow' from the hospital. My bag is a monster to drag on and off the pitch at high speed but that is my fault for ordering it and then filling it. With all the kit I have, the most popular item is a tiny pair of scissors that I stole from home as part of a tiny medical bag for walkers and runners, and I have had for years.

At the start of one particular game I wandered into the guys changing room meeting the usual banter and the obligatory loud and impossibly trendy dance music. I was greeted to the usual welcome.

"Hi Doc" came the chorus.

"Don't call me Doc, just Simon will do."

I have always squirmed at the term 'Doc': I don't know why.

"OK Doc" replied Les Davies our centre forward.

Cue general laughter at my expense. Since then, the name Doc stuck to me like chewing gum to the bottom of a shoe.

Bangor

Fiddler's Dram sang about their day trip to Bangor but unless you live there not many people know much about what Bangor gets up to. I am talking about the one in North Wales, not in County Down or for that matter another one in Maine, USA. And before you say, Bangor-on-Dee in Wrexham doesn't count as it has a different name. Bangor in North Wales is within the county of Gwynedd (pronounced with a 'th' at the end) and nestles between the eastern end of the Menai Strait and Snowdonia so has most of the Irish Sea tipped on it almost all year long thanks to a prevailing westerly wind. They say every cloud has a silver lining, but in Wales every cloud has about 100 other malevolent cloud friends with it, just full of water and no lining, silver or otherwise. They all pop along for a day trip to Bangor.

Admittedly, the city is picturesque in places but sadly it is often wet if not under water. It is trying its best to become Atlantis. Bangor is the sort of place you zoom past to, and from, your holidays in Anglesey or elsewhere in North Wales but without caring to stop. However, I think Bangor has a lot of charm. I consider most of the inhabitants of Bangor to be welcoming, unassuming and quite unexpectedly laid back. If a job can be left until tomorrow it may as well be done next week or not at all. That means on the other hand, it can be a bit irritating if you need something doing.

Bangor is the oldest city in Wales, housing 18,000 fair souls. It has a tiny cathedral. The cathedral is no York Minster or Saint Paul's but it was consecrated over a thousand years ago and it has a unique quaint charm and homely modesty. The original site of Bangor dates back to the time of the ancient Celtic saint Deiniol in the sixth century AD, and was based on a monastic site and then a Norman keep. There are no remains of either that have survived to the present day.

There is a cool ancient looking Gorsedd stone circle near Siliwen Road close to the strait. The stones are quite small, I would guess about as tall as a person with a flat stone in the middle. I was surprised to discover that the stone circle is not so ancient and was constructed for the National Eisteddfod in 1971. Apparently, they are built for each Eisteddfod which is at a different place in Wales every year, so they are pretty common too. The 1876 faithful may still wish to draw upon its potential and not so obvious pagan powers before difficult games. There will be difficult games ahead. Bangor has the National Trust owned Penrhyn Castle and garden close by, as well as the 2022 National Piers Society award winning Garth Pier with its onion dome topped spectacular Pier Pavillion Tea Room. The city is surrounded by a thriving farming community. There is a small fishing industry centred in Dickies Boatyard and Bangor is famous for its large succulent mussels.

Famous sons of Bangor are the singers Aled Jones and Sir Bryn Terfel. Although Aled was born in Bangor, and was discovered as a singing prodigy as a chorister at Bangor Cathedral, his childhood home was in Anglesey. Sir Bryn is really from Pant Glas on the Llŷn Peninsula which is the bit of spare mountain range left over from Snowdonia that juts out into the Irish Sea just like Michelangelo's finger of God gloriously adorning the ceiling of the Sistine Chapel, which, incidentally is not to be confused with that hand of God which was definitely not the work of Michelangelo, but of Maradona as he fingered the ball past a startled Peter Shilton so knocking England out of the 1986 World Cup. I am old enough to remain traumatised by that incident. Bangor has a famous daughter, Duffy. Like Aled Jones, Duffy was born in Bangor, but as a child and young woman lived on the Llŷn Peninsula. Predictably for Wales, all three are singers.

The main sources for employment for Bangor are with its university, and the local health services. These two worlds collided when Bangor 1876 approached Bangor University to use their pitch facilities and several people from the University Health Board became involved in the foundation of the new football club. I too, became involved in this partnership as a late comer to the party. So how did Bangor 1876 come about?

The collapse of Bangor City FC and the birth of Bangor 1876

Bangor has a long and proud history of association football as the name Bangor 1876 suggests. At one point, Bangor City was the fifth biggest team in the Welsh pyramid system behind Cardiff, Swansea, Newport and the Hollywood boys from Wrexham. Bangor City played in the English leagues until 1992 alternating between the fifth and sixth tiers of what are now the Vanarama National League and the Vanarama National League North. In 1978, Bangor City was scheduled for election to the English league but failed as its ground was inferior to that of Wigan Athletic who were promoted in place of Bangor. In 1984, Bangor made an appearance at Wembley in the non-league FA Cup but lost to Northwich Victoria in a replay. By then Bangor City was the biggest non-league team in Wales.

The Football Association of Wales (FAW) decided to start a national Welsh League in 1991 to protect the independence of the Welsh national football team within the Federation Internationale de Football Association (otherwise known as FIFA). Cardiff and Swansea were not invited, but Bangor agreed to take part after a degree of arm-twisting, as Bangor City were participating at that time within the English non-league system, whilst dealing with financial pressures of success in attracting bigger footballer salaries as well as other costs.

Bangor City were recurrent Welsh Cup winners and Welsh League champions with regular, albeit brief, forays into Europe with magical days to remember for the faithful of the old inner-city ground at Farrar Road and subsequently at Nantporth on the edge of the Menai Strait. In the early 1990s, Bangor City were Welsh Premier League champions on two occasions. Like many small clubs, City's financial difficulties were never far beneath their glory strewn exterior. Financial pressures continued and Bangor City's ground at Farrar Road was sold to Bangor City Council in the 1990s. There was further glory for Bangor City when they won the Welsh Cup three times in the noughties, qualified for European football and received prize money that should have resolved their financial woes. A final league title followed in 2011 with a last game win against Total Network Solutions, the big Welsh team of the day, yet based in England and nowadays known as The New Saints of Oswestry Town and Llansantffraid Football Club, with a crowd of 4000 to witness the historic day. Fortunately, Total Network Solutions' new team name became known as 'The New Saints' pretty quickly, which I think is a little easier to say and remember. Bangor found themselves in the Champions League and travelled to Helsinki only to receive an almighty thrashing. The move to Nantporth followed six months later and management costs escalated. A Welsh Cup final defeat to Prestatyn didn't help and by 2016 debts became insurmountable.

In 2017, a group of Cheshire-based businessmen made an offer to buy the club that was too good to be true, and if something appears to be too good to be true, normally it is just that. Bangor City supporters were concerned about financial irregularities and a lack of communication due to poor club management. In 2019, a new president and sole director of the club was appointed but debts and court cases continued. Salaries were not paid to players. Financial irregularities attracted the attention of S4C and the BBC News.

Where did this sad chain of events leave the Bangor faithful? First of all, let us scroll back a century when a supporters' group was formed and when association football was re-started after the First World War. This group was called the 'Bangor Comrades'. In 1919, Bangor City was temporarily renamed the Bangor Comrades and won the second-tier league title. The name then changed again to Bangor Athletic and then Bangor City in the 1930s. Adding the word 'comrades' was an acknowledgement by many clubs in North Wales to those who had given their lives in the Great War. They became the fan base for the predecessor of Bangor City in the inter-war years but then disappeared from view only to re-emerge when Bangor City FC were getting into their recent, and public, financial difficulties. They became an underground vigilante movement in the ensuing difficult times for Bangor City, distributing information and corralling discontent amongst the broader group of supporters of the club. The Comrades are an important part of our story that we shall revisit later. Secondly, as a result of poor community engagement and financial difficulties, the cost of Nantporth and growing concerns around the ownership of the club, many supporters sought to leave Bangor City despite its rich history and start another club where fans could have a say in its management. This new club was to have the principle of one share for each fan, regardless how much money they put into the new club. Finally, debts caught up with Bangor City in 2022 when the club was barred from footballing activities until all financial arrears were paid. Such sad events are always a disaster for any club and the community it serves.

An alternative was sought whilst poor Bangor City was a sinking ship foundering in stormy seas. It was not the fate a great and proud club football deserved. Bangor 1876 was developed by fans with a poor opinion of the management at Bangor City, and the vast majority of these were members of the Bangor City Supporters Association. Quickly a clutch of enthusiasts provided the managerial nucleus for the team as an action to secure the future of football in Bangor.

The core fan base formed the Bangor Football Supporters Society as a 'community benefit society', a fan owned community club with each member having a say in daily management and a vote at each annual general meeting with the intention of overcoming the poor relationship the management of Bangor City had experienced with its supporters in recent years. 1876 has around 400 members and allows supporter and community influence in the running of the club. It aims to support a number of charitable causes. There are board positions for enhanced volunteer roles. There are partnerships to develop services with Bangor University, Gwynedd Council, Bangor City Council and the FAW.

Why 1876? This was the name the supporters overwhelmingly accepted during a meeting in April 2019 and 1876 was an acknowledgement of the first football club in Bangor being formed as a commitment to its local community, following a meeting in Bangor in December 1876. Glynne Roberts, my friend who rang me about the club doctor post and a recently retired health service manager, was a director at Bangor City FC. He was appointed Chairman of the newly constituted football club. All those appointed to the board of 1876 were committed Bangor City fans and so the pain of the previous years' failings clearly runs deep. Six weeks later, Bangor 1876 was officially registered with the FAW to begin life in the lowest tier of Welsh league football. This was accepted as a giant leap of faith that has been found to be fully vindicated over the following seasons. Glynne has an eye on the bigger picture for where the club fits in its support of the local community and in the county of Gwynedd in North West Wales.

Les Pegler, a retired bank manager, Rob Lewis who is also retired and has a finance and management background and Robin Williams who is a financial advisor as well as Jonathan Ervine, Head of Modern Languages at Bangor University, linesman, long distance runner and our match reporter all gave their spare time to get things going. And so did a bunch of other supporters that I will return to in good time.

The biggest stroke of luck was to appoint Mel Jones as manager who had good local footballing contacts, and as he ran the junior academy at Bangor City, he knew all the best young talent. A longstanding Bangor City favourite, the centre-forward Les Davies, was asked to join who in turn asked if another talisman, the ex-Bangor defender Michael Johnston could come along too. Other players followed.

A scratch team played another fan-owned club, FC United from Manchester and it appeared a highly appropriate match-up for our first game, although losing

12-1 there was that one goal and around 400 of our spectators who together became the beating heart of the new club. *The Daily Post* reported with the headline on 12th July, 2019: "Bangor 1876 take to the field for the first time in landmark fixture". And then continues: "Phoenix club Clwb Pel Droed Bangor 1876 took the field for the first time this weekend as they took on FC United of Manchester. The Gwynedd League side travelled for their first friendly outing of the summer, and the newly formed, fan-owned club participated in a fabulous occasion both on-and-off the pitch... the visiting faithful were given a moment to savour a minute from time when talented teenager Benn Lundstram produced a moment of magic to go down in the history books as 1876's first ever goal scorer."

In truth the newborn baby Bangor had its bottom slapped, but in good faith, as it was time to take that all-important first breath.

John Dexter Jones, the 1876 club writer (amongst other attributes) and Bangor Comrade for the modern era, writes with pride when they played their first game against FC United: "For years, this feeling has been sucked away by the leeches that attached themselves to our club, our blue blood drained to the point of despair until some good people took a few soundings, then some tentative steps and then appropriately, in this year of moon-landing commemoration, a giant leap. We haven't built our own ground yet – we've been a football club for one month and one day – but who knows what we'll do. We've been a football tribe for much, much longer. The past belongs to generations of Citizens stretching back to 1876 – the future belongs to us. We are Bangor. The city is ours."

An unknown bard penned a limerick for Bangor 1876 and won a National Limerick Day competition organised by

Supporters Direct Europe in 2020 and so has become our first European success. Hopefully it will not be our only one. A good start to raise hopes for a bright future:

> "We play near the Menai Strait,
> The atmosphere really is great.
> Owned by fans,
> We've exciting plans,
> The return of football we await."
>
> *Anon*

One senior men's team, women's and girls' teams and four junior boys' teams have been set up with the women's and girls' teams being a club in their own right but sit as part of the 1876 burgeoning empire. By 2026, there are plans to have the female and youth teams to be fully engaged in the amateur Welsh league structure. A website and social media spread the gossip and news updates. An all-weather pitch was rented from Bangor University and quickly the standard of facilities demonstrated a clear intention for Bangor 1876 to progress through the lower leagues in Wales.

An identity for the club was needed. The longstanding Bangor coat of arms was taken as a reproduction of the ancient Welsh diocese called the See of Bangor from 1512. The significance of the mace, the two stars, the kneeling dragon at the top of the shield and the colours is not known. The dragon has a place in Welsh folklore although the exact origins are again unclear. Early Welsh kings used a dragon as a symbol of superiority over the retreating Romans in the fifth Century AD and later King Cadwaladr of Gwynedd used a red dragon symbol. The dragon's name of 'Y Ddraig Goch' literally means the red dragon in Welsh but has gained a more affable name Dewi in recent years. This is the Welsh equivalent for David and is a fit with the national day for Wales on 1st of March, St David's Day in honour of another Dewi, a sixth Century bishop of St David's in Pembrokeshire. Who would have thought that a great fire breathing monster terrorizing the wild Cambrian mountains and barren moors could be called Dave? Only the Welsh could do that.

Permission was granted to use the City of Bangor coat of arms as the club crest for 1876 with the team colours of blue and red taken from the colours of the coat of arms. A bit like Barcelona. But only just a bit. Their first team kit may be red and blue but the Barcelona coat of arms is yellow, red and white. No Dave and their coat of arms is a totally different shape, so overall, I think the Barca coat of arms is far less grand and fearsome compared to the coat of arms for our team. Admittedly both Barcelona and 1876 are similar in that they have had a taste of success. For Barcelona that has meant multiple national league titles and Champions League glory. For 1876 to date it has meant a prize-winning limerick. From small acorns…

The Bangor 1876 shirt was inspired by the football shirt Bangor City wore when they beat Napoli 2-0 at Farrar Road in 1962 in the European Cup Winners' Cup. This was royal blue with red trim. Now we have a name and we have a look.

Returning to John Dexter Jones: "Once you understand what football means to a community, you've cracked it. Some never will and they are condemned to live in a grim twilight of ducking, diving and discord". He continues: "There are no commercial certainties for Bangor 1876, just hard yards and hope. The people who are doing the hard yards are the ones who are offering that glimpse of hope. The rest of it is up to the tribe and the lads who wear the shirt."

Next, we needed an attitude. That came the following season.

The team doing what it does best: scoring goals. A suitably dejected goalie in the background. Picture courtesy of Matt Johnson.

The first season

Bangor 1876 needed some game time and the club accepted that it would have to begin life in the lowliest echelon of Welsh Football. Their first game was away against Ogwen Tigers with Bangor winning 4-1. Results like that continued and life in the North Wales Coast West Football League Division One turned out to be a confidence boosting first season winning the league by 10 points after winning all their league games. Bangor's biggest win was against Bethesda producing a towering scoreline of 14-0. Bangor ended the season with 116 goals scored, although this figure varies slightly from report to report but there were only nine conceded. They passed the 100-goal mark during a 6-0 win away to Caergybi (or Holyhead if you don't speak Welsh). Jamie Petrie was voted the players' player of the year. Match attendance was amazing from the start with around 400 attending for each game dwarfing the numbers attending for most opposition teams.

Grassroots North Wales reported: "Fan-owned Bangor 1876 comes out as the No1 supported non-league side playing in the Welsh system and makes the top 10 of non-league teams not based in England".

Speaking to *AFE Football News* at the season's end, Mel Jones the manager for that first season provided an erudite summation of his feelings: "It's a great achievement, especially when you think that twelve months ago the team hadn't even been formed. It's a credit to the management, board, players and fans that we've been able to work together throughout the season. It's been great the way local businesses and the local community in general have really got behind us." He added: "During the season, you could see the togetherness of the squad with the experienced players passing on their footballing knowledge to the younger players on and off the field. The younger players really benefited from this, and it helped to create a real sense of camaraderie within the squad." And he concluded: "Our fans have been absolutely outstanding, supporting us home and away in great spirits".

Such a commanding season instilled into 1876 an attitude of expecting hard work to provide an opportunity for the club to climb through subsequent leagues. But out of the blue Covid struck and Bangor 1876's first season was concluded six weeks early. The league positions at that point were accepted as the final league positions. The entire subsequent year of football was lost, and in the summer of

2021, when lockdown rules were being lifted, the team had to re-group and go again; this time in the fourth tier of Welsh football, the North Wales Coast West Football League Premier Division. This was when I received that fateful invitation from the chairman, Glynne Roberts.

My first home game

Saturday afternoon of the 10th July 2021 was mostly an overcast day but a calm introduction to life in a football club for the first cup game of the season, and the first in my official capacity as the club doctor. It was a great opportunity for me to get under the skin of a football club to see how all levels of organisation work on and off the pitch. This seemed an entirely different experience to watching the Premier League super clubs from row Z of huge stadiums or on TV. Turnstiles were absent and substituted by a collapsible table with two gents taking tickets.

"Four pounds please."

"I've been invited as the club doctor".

"Oh, OK Doc, then you are free mate".

I felt mean not having to fork out my four quid but never look a gift horse in the mouth, as they say. 'They' are presumably people who give horses away and I guess must be well minted. Those receiving the horses may be less so and may be thinking of eating their gifts but maybe I am reading too much into this.

The ground at Treborth looked impressive with floodlights, a high surround fence and a licenced clubhouse. Fans could watch from two of the four sides of the ground and there was a single small stand for 100 spectators called the 'Vera Owen Stand' as a token gesture of protection against the elements of which we know there are many in Bangor. Vera was a lifelong supporter of Bangor City and latterly of Bangor 1876. Sadly, she passed away recently. Spectator numbers were restricted to 100 for this game due to the Coronavirus restrictions imposed at the time. How quickly we forget the bad old days of the pandemic. This was no Old Trafford or Camp Nou but the small clutch of fans scattered around the ground was noisy and was intent on having a party. None were more than 10 feet from the touchline. Say something complimentary and you will often be rewarded with an acknowledgement from the players. Criticisms must be accurate as they are heard by all. I was pleased to be invited to join the festive atmosphere.

I noticed with interest that Treborth had an artificial pitch. This meant that the ball bounced high but ball control on the floor was predictable. But it looked perfect, bright green and even glistening in the occasional sunshine just like Lake Padarn on that sunny afternoon in Llanberis.

We took a comfortable win in what was billed as a qualifying round of the Welsh Cup, beating our local derby neighbour, Menai Bridge Tigers 8-2, with Chris Jones our in-form forward bagging four goals after his hat-trick the week before. Both sides were awarded a penalty each, both of which were converted. Bangor and Menai Bridge had bright starts to the league season but Bangor were set to continue with their good form to consolidate its league position towards the top of the table. Dyl Williams, the first team manager for the start of this second season had indeed instilled a winning attitude.

As it happened, there were no major injuries and Trudy, the physio, was happy to sort the knocks and stretches whilst introducing me to the science of sports injuries. Rhys hadn't started with us at this early stage of the season. A lot of listening was the order of the day between cheering the many goals. I was busy sorting medical forms for our players in order to see who had allergies or chronic conditions needing medication. A few weeks earlier in Copenhagen, Christian Eriksen collapsed from a cardiac arrest during the Denmark-Finland game in the Euros. That came as an eerie warning shot across the bows, as already my focus was to look at serious injury management by developing a head injury protocol borrowed from both the World Rugby Head Injury Assessment and the FA Concussion Guidelines, and checking out the use of the nearest defibrillator near the changing rooms, heaven forbid should we ever have to use it.

Whilst an impressive win was entertaining for me as a spectator and dare I say it, not as yet morphed into a fan, the day was uneventful as far as injuries were concerned with both teams surviving to fight another day. But there was a player who instantly caught my eye.

Johno

God so loved Bangor that he gave his only son and his son was Johno. Given that He realised Johno wasn't quite perfect, He gave the good citizens of Bangor 22 more, and lo they became Bangor 1876. He was pleased. This massive birth explosion did require a lot of room at a lot of local inns. They have been full ever since, and there has been no room for any wise men.

There is a clutch of Bangor City stalwarts who have seen a new beginning at Bangor 1876 and have been patient enough to start with a club at the lowest tier of the Welsh football league. Included in that select group is Michael Johnston or Johno as he is unimaginatively but affectionately known. He played for some years as the premier centre back in Welsh football, but the need to supplement a modest income from his part-time football involved him gaining a sound academic education and becoming a primary school teacher. A leader full of revered opinions, whether welcome or otherwise, made him a natural choice as the first team manager after a rather unexpected parting of the ways with the previous manager, Dyl, mid-season. Always encouraging in seeing the choreography of the game, Johno can identify weaknesses in the opponents and develop strategies for good defence and goal scoring opportunities.

Johno arrived on this planet not in Bethlehem but Merseyside in the year that *The Simpsons* first aired on TV, and when personal computers and cell phones were introduced as the great new future; but they both weighed a ton and cost a bomb. He was born when the Pet Shop Boys were top of the charts with *Always on my mind*. The boy Johnston has always been on the minds of the Bangor faithful since the day he turned up at Bangor City about 15 years ago. Previously he was in the Tranmere Rovers youth system and played for the Wales under-17 and under-19 teams. Short, slightly bow legged and the stocky build of a seasoned pro, Johno has the cheeky Charlie persona of a scouse version of Robbie Williams. No singer he, but the receiver of many a crooning football fan's adulation. Johno's small flashing eyes and quick wit would always deliver a salvo of advice, mixed with thinly veiled threats, directed with a laser glance that would strike with the accuracy of a cruise missile. You do as he says without question.

Rare picture of Johno sporting a smile captured by Dafydd Hughes using a short exposure time.

Johno's inclusive method of leadership on the pitch made the move into football management a natural progression. He has a Union of European Football Associations (UEFA) B licence but is working towards a pro-licence so that games can be held in Europe with him as the club manager. You can see where his ambitions lie. It was a steep learning curve when he took over as manager at Bangor 1876 and, with a new baby at home, he had many new responsibilities. Always professional, seemingly never letting the heavy weight of duties get the better of him, his enjoyment of what is not a job but what he sees as a hobby is obvious. His pet hates are refs who don't listen and the bad mouthing from other teams who consider 1876 a rich team, who illegally pay their players, and so should win and consider that 1876 are not doing as well as they should. He sees jealousy from other teams obsessed with what is happening at the club. Johno is annoyed further when this jealousy can be taken out on the fans. He has never shown any lack of courtesy to other teams and expects the same high standard of behaviour in return.

Johno can play still, if needed, though recurrent injuries have deprived him of his previous agility. During the sunny

Llanberis game Tom Clarke, our centre half, was getting cramp. Johno stripped off, warmed up and was ready to replace the struggling young defender.

"I'm OK boss" yelled Tom.

Johno's face dropped. More cramp.

"I think I can carry on."

"Tom – stop toying with my emotions!"

Johno didn't get an opportunity to play that day.

On another occasion our midfielder Harry Galleotti, or 'H' for short, was breaking down the right wing ready to receive a pass so he was looking at the ball; not where he was going. As he raced past an onlooking Johno, who was standing outside his technical area, and slightly encroaching onto the pitch, H tripped over Johno's foot so falling flat on his face and slid to a halt. Everybody, including H, were laughing with the referee letting slip a broad grin, as H slowly picked himself up whilst attempting to work out how to retrieve some dignity from the situation. Johno quickly retreated from the scene of the crime.

"Aye what does that mud taste like, H?" Johno mused.

There was no response from H. But, of course actions speak louder than words. Sure enough a few moments later, H again broke down the same wing, this time with the ball, accelerated past an opposition defender and whipped in a curling cross for Corrig to head gratefully into the back of the net to rapturous cheers. Johno had some advice.

"Hey, H – see what you can do when you stay on your feet!"

Johno's passion for the game is unparalleled.

Johno has his heart in the Bangor community too as he started regular matchday food bank collections after noting similar work in Liverpool with 'Fans Supporting Foodbanks'. He sees the essential community role of the club for the city of Bangor. He considers that the support of the community is intrinsic to the club. Before Covid in the first season, fans were asked to bring donations to support a food bank in Bangor. This was seen as strictly optional as some fans could have been users of that food bank and Johno wished that all were felt to be welcome.

I had a chance to catch up with Johno to talk about his obvious commitment to Bangor 1876. I was interested in how he managed to find time to manage a football club, have a family life with a new baby and fit in a day job as a teacher. He said he always had the support of his wife but travelling to Bangor, and elsewhere, with his football was always part of his life for at least a day a week. There can be long days for the games in the deepest depths of Wales but it was second nature to travel and play football.

Why has he displayed such loyalty to Bangor City and then to 1876? This appears to be because Johno enjoys the ongoing respect he has earned over the years to ease his transition from player to manager. He has always been comfortable being with both Bangor City and Bangor 1876. He sees the strengths of 1876 in being a bunch of lads who primarily enjoy their football, he aims to get as high in the Welsh League as possible and constantly improve team spirit to help each other when times are tough. Also, he believes that ongoing success tends to pull the team together for all to develop in the same direction. This is the confidence bred from winning, so developing a winning mentality. The club is run by its fans and Johno is happy to run the team as long as the fans want that. There are no egos to massage and no conflicting personalities. That is so refreshing to hear.

I asked how all those around him could make his life better. He felt this could be achieved by all staff pulling together as a team for the common good. Fans have a huge wealth of experience to bring to the team and to the club. Some help with the day to day commitments and they gladly give up their free time to do so. He finished by adding that more sponsors are always useful which would be pretty handy as that seems to be the main way to add to income to deal with the inevitability of rising costs. Income from gate receipts is not likely to increase at present. So that is where the board needs to help.

My FAW first aider course

It seems that six years at medical school and 13 years of pretty rigorous postgraduate training on the wards to become a consultant wasn't good enough to be a club doctor for the FAW. I had to attend a first aider course. So, one evening in the autumn in 2021, Dafydd Hughes kindly paid for me to attend a basic first aider course at Conwy Football Club. That was pretty handy as Conwy is only a five-minute drive from my house.

I rock up to these sort of training events always with the same feeling of trepidation that I could be made to look foolish by not knowing answers to some basic questions in front of non-medical people. However, the course leader and the other attendees seemed friendly enough. Yet a potential deep hole opened for me immediately which blew away my anonymity. Following our introductions, the course leader asked how many cardiac arrests we had attended. I knew that this was going to go badly for me. He soon rumbled that I was a doctor when I seemed to have been to more arrests than all of the other attendees and the course leader combined. I had more deaths on my hands than I really wanted to admit to: but that was just the job I did. A year as a house doctor, that is the most junior doctor of the lot, sometime deep into the last century, fresh faced and just released from university upon an unsuspecting public, gave me a baptism of fire when I seemed to work more hours than there were hours in the week. That meant a lot of running with a crash trolley and zapping a lot of folks and doing a lot of cardiopulmonary resuscitation or CPR. Then followed a quick coffee, many biscuits, exchanging a few poor taste jokes and then off the next arrest. Anyhow, as those days were long ago, and apart from my mandatory training refreshers which lasted about an hour per year, I had little recent experience of the do's and don'ts of resuscitation and of basic first aid. A further update would do me no harm.

We began by covering what we needed to put into a tiny first aid kit which I already possessed and I was pleased that at least I could tick that box. But I didn't quite possess everything I needed. Embarrassingly, as I am a gynaecologist, I had no tampons to stuff bleeding noses. That was one job for me. I know I will get embarrassed when I go to the chemist and ask for a box of tampons. Wrong age; wrong gender. They'll think I must be a wierdo. Then I realised that as a gynaecologist I had never fitted a tampon and had to read the instructions. I was determined that I wasn't going to make a complete arse of myself on pitch. How difficult could it be? I guess you stuff it in the right place at arm's length, and just like a flare pull the string and close your eyes. As long as no smoke comes out I should be OK.

Then we were usefully shown how to use an Epipen or an adrenaline auto-injector for anaphylaxis as I had not used one before. There is usually rubber crumb in artificial pitches, but all gloves used by Rhys, Trudy and I are latex free. I have a list of our players' allergies but I have no details of the opposition teams or of the match officials. Apparently, there is a risk that if you hold the wrong end of the Epipen you could inject yourself instead of the intended victim. 'Blue-end to sky' is the phrase to avoid calamity. The adrenaline hit would be like a succession of double expresso coffees making you manic for a few hours. Not good. Although, following your accidental self-immolation there is a chance that you might find yourself doing every outstanding chore that previously you had kicked into the long grass, and so there is a remote chance of benefit. That meant there was another job for me; to get some Epipens.

Next, I was also reminded of the recovery position, for the unconscious person to be laid on their side, both arms bent in front of the head with the upper hand below the face and the hip and knee of the upper leg also bent to keep the patient secure in that position. All good tips.

Players, especially our junior trainees, like to choke. On gum shields, bubble gum or pen and bottle tops. Grapes and mini-eggs are always a risk apparently so should be avoided at sporting events. I have never tried a Heimlich manoeuvre before, this is where the blue choking unfortunate is given an almighty bear hug from behind. Don't try that in a Caernarfon pub on the Saturday night or you'll get thumped. Blows to the back can be tried first in the hope the offending object can be coughed out. Beware, as even that will still get you thumped anywhere in Caernarfon. Being the pessimist that I am, I decided to put together my own on-pitch tracheostomy set using a large bore drip needle and added it to my mega-bag. My medical kit was becoming a mini emergency department.

CPR is always fun to practise, but much more stressful in real life. We were always reminded to ask for help, check your ABC which is not for the first aider to have alcohol, a banana and chocolate before summoning Dutch courage (possible a 'D') for the task ahead but to check the unconscious person's airway, their breathing and circulation or pulse. This management pathway will help decide whether mouth to mouth only is needed or whether full CPR with chest compressions are required. Checking the airway involves ensuring the mouth is clear with a careful look: sometimes the tongue can flop back towards the throat. I am wary that any prying finger inserted into the victim's mouth can be bitten at this point: therefore, looking is better but sometimes a small plastic airway, which is like a gum shield with a tube to allow air in and out, can be inserted into the mouth if there is an airway available. Vomit is a bit of a downer if mouth to mouth is needed. So, with all that in mind we had a go with CPR, thankfully not on each other but on special training dollies. Which don't vomit. Or bite.

Finally, we moved to the defib machine or give it its real name the Automated External Defibrillator or AED for short. This is what is needed if there is a Christian Eriksen moment. It is easy to use, at least it was on the first aider course, but I have not come into contact with one of these in real life before. All that is required is just to follow the instructions and remember whilst you are resuscitating someone, a second person is needed with a mobile to go to fetch the AED and to ring the number advertised by the secured AED in order to get a release code so it can be removed from its mounting and taken to the scene of the event. Oh, and don't forget to have a third person to phone for an ambulance PDQ.

I duly received my certificate, Dafydd was happy that the FAW recognised my evening's hard but enjoyable work and that I had become an official first aider for the club. I must admit that I am quite proud of my piece of paper as I feel the club has invested in me and in my role. I am also grateful for the course leader remaining civil with me. I tried to hide my medical expertise but that lasted all of five minutes. I did gain lots of useful practical tips.

Capturing the beauty of the beautiful game

Creative opportunities abound in a sports setting. Of course, in Wales the singing and poetic chants from a football crowd could become an Eisteddfod in every game. 1876 is no exception and with true artistic verve we have Llion Jones as our resident poet. Not too many clubs have one of those. Llion composed a collection of poetry called *Bardd ar y bêl*, which literally means 'poet on the ball' describing the Welsh national team on their impressive run at the Euros in 2016, where they ultimately progressed to the semi-final. Perfect for us. He won the bardic chair at the 2000 National Eisteddfod. This is awarded to the best poetry written as 'cynghanedd' (meaning harmony), which is a harmonic writing style of verse. He is a director at the Welsh Language Unit at Bangor University and a supporter of Bangor 1876.

The artisan trio is completed with Pete Jones as our resident associate artist and John Dexter Jones as our writer. John has another string to his bow as he is a singer so I suspect a Welsh choir is in the offing. Furthermore, I think 1876 would expect a terrace ditty somewhat more stylish than *Nice one Cyril*. What about something along the lines of *Nessun Dorma* for the tenors in the crowd and I stress I am not one of those. I can't wait. John also is self-described as a moiderer (this seems to be some form of local verbal affliction to which I have dedicated a chapter) as is Pete; a football fan and mountain punk (I haven't quite worked out what that is but it sounds a tad subversive and scary). His interests are the arts, mental health and 1876. As John saw it with Bangor City in crash and burn mode, the best way to ensure that there was to be local football was to break away to form a new not-for-profit local club to ensure Bangor regained a functional local team. Whilst Pete and John found themselves journeying through a grieving process over the implosion of Bangor City, the pair had the idea to re-form the old Bangor Comrades to keep the flame going via Facebook in sharing stories of football in Bangor whilst Bangor City struggled. This preceded the inaugural meeting of Bangor 1876.

The Comrades subsequently became the unofficial supporters' group for 1876 and have financially, and personally, supported a mental health drop-in centre through sales of their unique branded Bangor 1876 football shirts and with other activities. Pete was a mental health nurse and his influence led to the local Abbey Road mental health drop-in centre being selected for financial support, which is a valuable resource for the local community. This decision followed the death of a friend due to mental health problems. The Comrades accept that men are particularly vulnerable to the effects of depression, and other mental health issues, largely because of a difficulty in expressing their feelings and an inability to seek help when it is needed.

From an article in the *North Wales Chronicle* of 1st December 2021, the work of the Bangor Comrades was summarised succinctly: "Pete and John are both associate artists at Bangor 1876, whose role within the club is to promote the positive benefits of football in the community through the medium of the arts".

The Chronicle further reports an interview with Pete Jones: "As a fan-owned club, 1876 strives to play a positive role within the local community. It wants to bring people together in many more ways than simply watching a game.

We want to promote a spirit of togetherness for the benefit of the wider community through projects like this."

Other creative developments include the production of a music CD and a publication of poems within a portfolio of activities as part of a project called Comradiation, with further releases and possible live events supporting the Abbey Road mental health drop-in centre. *Comradiation* is also the name of a CD to which local artists contributed their music. All are former Bangor City fans too.

The online Bangor newspaper, *The Bangor Aye*, reported the Comrades' activities. "Comradiation – Abbey Road, is a compilation album of music from artists in the Bangor area, or who have a strong connection with the city. Some have supplied previously unreleased material, whilst others have written songs specifically for the project."

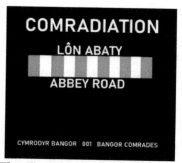

The Comradiation CD cover.

There are others who strive to spread the good name of 1876. Our camera men for all games are Matt Johnson and Dafydd Hughes who are always creeping around, usually at diametrically opposed ends of the pitch, incognito or so they think, attempting to capture unguarded expressions of the players and not to startle their unsuspected subjects.

Both have different techniques for stalking their prey but between them always produce detailed visual diaries of the progress of each, and every football game. These then appear on the 1876 website within a day or so. Matt happens to be a teacher in Abergele and has a penchant for following obscure teams around the world. And yes, he has a Dukla Prague away kit! It might be only the home top actually.

John writes of the first game of this season after a 12-month hiatus with a passion: "In all our lives these have been the most unexpected of times, the most challenging, and in many cases, the worst. We craved normality just as we knew that there was never any such thing; we wondered what was to come; we waited and waited and waited. Those working in healthcare and science and on buses and in shops and vaccination centres gave us a fighting chance. I have walked further than the Proclaimers. Over the Chiltern Hills and the mountains of Eryri, I have paced out my sanity and kept my distance. Thousands upon thousands of steps have passed, but the next fifty will take me into the one cage that I have ached to be inside. Ten greetings, twenty. Smiles and thumbs-ups. Catching up on eighteen months in eighteen seconds – the surreality begins to dissolve until I finally accept that I am here, this is happening and I'm leaning on the barrier to the right of the goal, and there's a game going on.

Matt discusses tenses for the live Tweets. I picture distant Comrades punching the air as the goals go in and the Tweets ping. They will join us when they can. I hear myself talking about the game. Tom Clarke could make one hundred-and-fifty-seven goal attempts today and he will not score. Culshaw, in space on the edge of the box, begs Les to set him up… or, when the pass doesn't come, in a stage whisper, says… "have a shot" after The Truck [Les] scuffs one straight at the keeper. We laugh. He looks. He smiles at the fact that we are as invested in this game as he is. Of course we are – some of us have been taking part in this theatre since long before he was born. Good player. Never stops. Neat and tidy. Fit as a butcher's dog.

At the end, we applaud both teams. Pentraeth will not win this league. We harbour that particular hope, but the distant, golden, Gwynedd League past is just that. As we leave the ground, somehow the statistics and the battles ahead are placed into context by the breezy, warm July here-and-now. It's been a cliché for decades to say that 'we never look further than the next game' but on this, the first day of the competitive season, it's haunting to think that we have no choice other than to hold tight to the present.

I've missed this more than I thought was possible."

Llion, Pete, John, Matt and Dafydd aim to spread the word of 1876 by bringing cultural influences into the club. Inspired by varied creative activities as well as the football at the inaugural game hosted by FC United in Manchester, some festive community activities normally seen outside the club are planned for match days. This is for the future. But I gather Northern soul, Ska and reggae music are on the agenda. Going to watch 1876 play will be like going to Wembley, the Barbican, the Albert Hall, the Tate and an Eisteddfod all at the same time. Wow! Now that will be worth seeing.

My pre-match prep

Most games are on a Saturday afternoon meaning an early lunch for me. I chuck some chocolate bars into my immense physio bag and once midsummer has been shown the door I dress as if I am going to the South Pole. In Bangor, and at many of the away grounds I have visited in North West Wales, perishingly cold winters seem to exist for the majority of the football season. Most days have a pretty challenging weather system heading our way if we are playing at home or away, and sadly some of these are bad enough to have names. So, I prepare for the worst.

Winter time is a time for an especially detailed routine. My usual lucky undies have not yet become part of my fledgling 1876 costume. I will be standing still for long periods of any game so thermal underwear is next, thick walking socks and waterproof walking pants. You can count on getting a good soaking in Bangor and in most places that we visit. Then a 'Bangor Comrades' T-shirt follows and of course my royal blue with red trim 1876 home first team top proudly completes the all-weather protection. Sometimes I add a woollen walking fleece. The difference between a high tide whizzing along the Menai Strait and a sudden deluge is a subtle one at Treborth and my half time coffee can be a life saver. There are so many layers I can barely bend. Still I reckon it is better to be too warm so I can peel layers off than be a shivering wreck in front of all these fit and healthy young men demonstrating their derring-do on the football pitch. I don't want to be seen quaking in the dugout in front of all the spectators. No one else in the dugout ever shivers for reasons I don't understand.

On most winter days I add a few condiments, with my waterproof walking shoes, gloves, 1876 scarf and 1876 bobble hat almost completing my strange ensemble. The final item is my Bangor 1876 royal blue coach's coat. Of all my bits and pieces, I am most proud of my blue coat as I ceremoniously slip my arms into it. It is quite padded so it almost stands up by itself and is really warm. It has the 1876 emblem on the left breast. But best of all it has my initials on it. 'SL'. My initials on the right breast. I feel so wanted and a part of the team with my SL. SL is added to cars that have a bit of an upgrade. Standard Luxury. That's me, standard with a bit of luxury thanks to my cushdie coat. The last time I had clothes with my name on I was at junior school. Then the Beatles topped the charts here and everywhere else and a man was taking small steps on the moon. Even better is that my coat hasn't got the word 'Doc' scrawled across the back. The coat was a kind gift from the management of 1876 and I must admit I expected those three letters somewhere when they did the big reveal. However, please note that the badge and my name are there for a reason: if I get lost in the wilds of Wales, a kindly member of the public may take pity on me and then return me (and my coat) safely back to Treborth. Finally; car keys – check; kit bag – check. I am good to go.

Then I have to take off the gloves, hat, scarf and coat so that I can fit into my car. My immense kit bag, and all the discarded clothing, are chucked into the boot and I'm off to the game. If only I knew where it was.

A day of reckoning

Despite having lived in North Wales for 25 years I hadn't heard of Bodedern. It is the sort of place hidden at the far end of Anglesey you could drive through in the blink of an eye. Closely packed grey houses lean toward each other for mutual support and to keep sunlight, but not the rain, from the streets. Occasional dogs wander around sullen, depressed and underfed. They are too tired to bark. There are people wondering about perhaps looking for shelter. Bodedern is a place that is clearly too small to have 11 young male inhabitants let alone having a team in Bodedern Athletic, which has been an outstanding beacon of consistency in winning every game up to this point, in our league. Bangor's palatial avenues in contrast have honed the aesthete X-men of our team, with well chiselled granite looks sculpted from the very mountains of Snowdonia. Surely the result of such a clash of titans versus a nondescript team is inevitable in favour of the glorious 1876. Such hubris can end only one way and indeed Bodedern had other ideas. They had a plan.

Since our seemingly unequal match-up, I have been wondering what happened that day and I decided that the likeliest explanation was that there must have been an, as yet unreported, alien landing in the uncharted fields of deepest Anglesey with the alien nation embarking on a cruel experiment to seed the local population with expert footballers in an attempt to seize world or, at least, FIFA domination. Bodedern seems a strange choice but I guess even aliens have to start somewhere. I confess I may have been overthinking this but it is possible that such experiments have been tried before with some success from alien pre-invasion scouting parties taking over at Chelsea and Manchester City, both teams previously existing as Premier League journeymen and transformed by mysterious forces into globetrotting monster mega-teams overnight. The official explanation was that rich people bought the clubs, rather than an extra-terrestrial experiment to which the FA may have objected, and also more plausibly, to prevent worldwide panic. And so, the scene was set.

Bangor 1876 was to visit Bodedern on this, a deeply grey, autumnal day. Saturday the 20th November was wet which followed several wet days. This day was wetter still. Daylight struggled to permeate through dense and angry clouds coming at us from each and every direction desperate to drop their watery payload as soon as they could. Even the sullen and depressed local dogs didn't want to go for their walks. Every-one was wet. We needed a pub stop on the treacherous journey from the pond that was a car park to the pond that was a football pitch. Having been invigorated by yet more liquid, our group, like the cast from the film *Waterworld*, solemnly paraded to the venue. My waterproof clothes had given up the overwhelming task at hand, and simply allowed me to become as wet as everywhere else as far as the eye could see. The pitch was predictably heavy with more mud than grass and the rain was unrelenting. I suspect that the weather was not part of Boded's plan but the home team adapted to the tumultuous conditions far better than us. The dad of Tom, our defender, cut a lonely figure taking his reluctant small dog around the ground. The puddles were so big, and the dog so small, that the poor beast had to wade through most of the challenging perimeter tour. This produced almost as much interest as watching the 22 players wandering around wishing that they were anywhere else but where they were. At times they were like fishermen manically keeping their boat afloat in a hurricane. Almost all fans, home and away were huddled in a single small stand which was clearly overfull, in the vain hope that the rain would take pity on us and fall elsewhere.

By half time Bangor were 1-0 down and repeatedly second to every free ball. We were beginning to get the picture that we had a game on our hands. Bodedern wanted to prove a point and the point was that Bangor would have to fight hard to win the league. However, our patience paid off and we looked a little brighter after the break. Dyl, the manager must have had a stern word with the boys. Chris Jones equalised from the spot early in the second half and Bangor took the lead on the hour, with a well taken goal from our midfielder Sion Edwards in open play. I reckoned it would be worth a total soaking if we bagged all three points. Surely the game was ours and our hopes began to rise. We just had to hold out for half an hour against the elements including what appeared to be most of the Irish Sea being thrown at us and, let us not forget, Bodedern Athletic. On the other hand, the prospect of victory must have seemed more remote for our opposition. But no. Two penalties awarded for rare defensive howlers by our boys sealed the tie in Boded's favour. Even so, the ensuing spot kicks for Boded were not so straightforward, given the apocalyptic conditions. Both were duly scooped from the puddle that was a penalty spot in better days to end up in another puddle in the back of our net. The 1876 faithful trudged home in a reflective mood and nothing to show for their thorough soaking.

So, the course of the rest of the season was set. Bodedern Athletic turned out to be ruthless in chalking up win after win to keep them top as well as providing a professional job of keeping us just out of harm's way before a scheduled show down towards the end of the season. Could we steal their intended glory? We would have to wait to find out during the following summer.

Being a medic only occasionally helps

The early part of the season was something of a baptism of fire for me, with our striker Gethin Thomas breaking his ankle away at Gaerwen. Sam Ashworth had a troublesome ankle strain and both were out for some months. There were a bunch of head injuries when two players attempted an unscheduled Glasgow hello, which were painful for the players but both recovered quickly and neither had to be substituted. I achieved a first in my outrageously long medical career, following another head injury, which happened away at a place called Mynydd Llandegai early in the season, when I was surprised to receive laughter from

47

my appreciative audience of fans after brilliantly applying a dressing to a scalp skin split. The player concerned had some bleeding above an eye brow but this only needed some pressure. I was rather pleased with my effort only to realise the player, who was the centre forward at Mynydd Llandegai, had a little unused bubble of dressing on the top of his head which made him and my dressing look like a monstrous condom. He was very polite to me, considering my pantomime efforts, but had to leave the pitch if only to stop the giggling from around the ground. Bugger. He remained unfeasibly forgiving considering what I had done to him.

Jonathan Ervine, our PR man was more objective in his report of the game: "Mynydd were somewhat hampered by injuries with scorer Osian Jones going off injured at half-time and his strike partner" he adds "having to leave the field wrapped in bandages after a head injury during the second period". Unlike me, at least you were professional Jonathan. "The injury," Jonathan continues "resulted in a lengthy stoppage and a significant amount of injury time being added on."

I have never been asked for an encore before but perhaps the injury time added on was not for the crowd to see me do more daft dressings but just to play out the time I had wasted in the first place. The lesson of that day was to know your bandages and if efforts are going a bit Pete Tong then, with the ref's permission, take the victim off the pitch for a few minutes out of the public gaze. Noted.

Following another game, Mark Hawkins, one of our goalies, required surgery for a broken wrist and missed the second half of the season. I wasn't involved in dealing with Mark's injury but all of these were a menagerie of relatively straightforward problems to sort out. Those I struggled with were the many various strains to the groins, hamstrings, quads, calves and ankle sprains. All of these appeared to me as wretchedly vague complaints but I had to admit, appeared painful and stopped our boys doing what they did best. These needed strapping and this part of the physio's role was where Rhys and Trudy introduced me to the mystical arts of adding blue tape, KT tape and cohesive bandage within the science of sports injuries. They also advised me about massage and stretches. Once again, YouTube proved helpful in giving instruction on the application of various tapes for various injuries, but still I remained mystified. There seemed to be several ways to skin a cat. Which was best? Fortunately for me, the players also knew how to dress their injuries and were quite forgiving with my efforts although Geth made me re-apply a dressing once to his slowly healing ankle injury. Though I have to admit he was polite enough to suggest that it was his fault for not guiding me sufficiently. Also, I had my trusty massage gun to manage some of the muscular injuries and this became useful to ease some of our defender Shaun Lock's various back strains. I have to clarify that Shaun did not require shooting however tempting this may have been over the season but the massage gun provided muscle stimulation with a rapid action massage pump. Shaun is heralded as the man with amazingly long, potent throw-ins and shots that regularly exceed the sound barrier though few are on target. Any goalie is advised to get body armour for those hammer blows that may be goal bound. On most match days, Johno needs his entire body sorting and may have been better off with a zimmer frame. The Lightweight Rollator 105 with the travel bag would have been my choice but other options are available at many stockists. Johno loves to play. He will keep getting himself into match fitness until his body cries 'no' that final time, and it is absolutely no longer possible for him to get on the pitch as a player for the first team. Then there was the issue of ice packs, Deep Freeze and Deep Heat. Which to use? When to use? I slowly learned that ice packs are good for acute injuries at the pitch side for players needing to be substituted. Deep Freeze is handy for players on the pitch that can continue. I must admit Deep Heat seems better after the game to get folks home with their analgesia but I suspect professionals reading this may have other ideas. Some players like Deep Heat before they start a game. Nonetheless, I am convinced that there should be no Deep Heat applied to the groins especially in hot weather lest I start a forest fire. I am still learning.

Rhys, Trudy and I still feel a switch away from the all-weather pitch at Treborth, and a greater use of warm-up and cool-down sessions before and after games, will help us to keep our lads away from various strains and sprains throughout the year. These are issues which are being reviewed at the club.

1876 had good form to keep notching up wins through the winter months to keep us in contention with Boded; but as the season progressed we still remained second favourites to gain that one and only vital promotion place to the next league. We were beginning to run out of time.

The end of the season approaches with Menai Bridge Tigers v Bangor

On Tuesday evening on 5th April, we enjoyed the closest rivalry in the UK which attracted the interest of the BBC. Jonathan managed to become a celebrity after being quoted by the Beeb: "We've not had an afternoon when we've both been playing simultaneously so we haven't interrupted each other's games yet". Time will tell.

Menai Bridge is a small town on Anglesey at the opposite end of the picturesque old iron Menai road suspension bridge designed by Thomas Telford which happens to have the mainland end just next to the long narrow drive to our ground at Treborth. Menai Bridge is a pretty enough place and even boasts a Waitrose which is well posh in itself, but it is *that* Waitrose which Kate and Wills regularly visited for their weekly shop when Prince William was learning to fly helicopters at RAF Valley at the far end of the island. Menai Bridge (the place not the bridge) has a rugby and a cricket club, but unfortunately it has no available ground large and flat enough for a football pitch. So, the Tigers, like us, rent a ground from the University.

Spring had threatened to push winter away but by early April, it was still chilly. At least it wasn't raining on the evening concerned.

Our local derby involved us walking 40 yards from our pitch at the University to the Tiger's pitch, which was still at the University but involving a relatively straightforward trek in the dark across a whole car park and a bit of a field. All away fans made it unscathed. As it was an away game, there was an entrance fee for me to pay. I forgot my wallet. I turned up with Glynne Roberts and Glynne had to fork out a hard earned four quid to get me into the game for which I apologised. A beer would be repayment for a later date. The floodlights were a bit politically correct, with our hosts using trendy University eco-friendly bulbs leaving a non-light polluted (or dark) pitch. This made ball skills a bit nuanced or something of a luxury. I parked myself in the dugout next to Rhys but in truth I was a bit of a spare part. Nonetheless, we had a tricky start with a fiery attack from the Tigers appropriately scaring us in their yellow and black striped kit, which led to a throw-in for us in our half, from which we scored. And scored again. Tom Clark and our attacker Les Davies both scored within five minutes. Indeed, after some rather precarious defending by Tigers, we were 5-0 up by the break. The players elected to stay out as the changing rooms were too far from the pitch. Alas, there was no water for the boys and so Glynne and I made the tricky journey back across the field, car park and around our pitch to our clubhouse and collected several plastic glasses and filled them with water from an outside standpipe. Now clinging on to several full glasses each of water, we precariously tootled back with water splashing in all directions, on a now slightly less straightforward journey around our home ground, across the car park and the field to the game. This reminded me of a mini marathon in the old TV series of 'Jeux Sans Frontières'. By the time we returned, exhausted, with water supplies reasonably intact and not too many splashes over our clothes, the second half had started. Sion Edwards or Sioned was subbed and he was so pissed off at his performance he threw one of his boots into our newly collected cups of water knocking most of them over like skittles. By the way, Sion is called Sioned so as not to be confused with our defender Shaun Lock whose nickname is, well, Shaun Lock. Sioned's nickname is really Sion Eds which would make far more sense but I realised this only at the end of the season. Sion always responded to Sioned when I spoke to him but maybe he just didn't hear me too well. Sioned is a Welsh girl's name meaning God's gift. Maybe Sioned would be more appropriate, apart from being a girl's name that is. Sioned suspected that I may have been disappointed when I shouted at him. He gave me a pained expression as if I had just stood on one of his freshly exposed feet. In fairness he shook his head and apologised instantly. He stopped sulking and tidied his boots away. The cups remained looking like a car crash with water dripping everywhere. At least we got something for him to throw his boot at.

Well with three points in the bag, the 1876s were able to play within themselves. Johno by then had become the first team manager and seemed to sub the entire team but we still scored another without reply from Menai Bridge. We were happy. Johno was confused why a substituted player was limping off the pitch.

"Oi, why are you limping, you've injured your wrist."
There was no response.

Irritatingly, our league topping rivals knocked in five in their game to Llanberis where we struggled to knock one past on that sunny Saturday just a few days before and so Boded were still five points up on us.

North Wales Coast West Football League Premier Division		
1 - Bodedern Athletic	played 23 games	67 points
2 - Bangor 1876	played 23 games	62 points

Now for the last five games. But we would have to wait for the end of a fortnight's Easter break which was just around the corner. At least Johno had time to go home and feed his newborn baby. He is the only team member who has to get up more often during the night than me, if only, perhaps, for a different reason.

Les the Truck

This story is as much a part of North Wales folklore as Johno being the son of the Almighty. Les Davies received a surprising nomination in 2012 when he was a Bangor City player. This resulted in widespread media coverage. The nomination was for the annual UEFA best player award and is presented by the European Football Association. The long list is chosen by football journalists. A rumour goes that a local journalist, Dave Jones, spotted that only 31 of the 32 nominations had been completed and thought of a worthy local star. Les is known as 'the Truck' for his physical prowess and had been at the top of his game within the Welsh Premier League for some years.

The *Daily Mirror* reported that: "semi-professional Bangor City striker Les Davies admits his inclusion on the list for a top UEFA honour is 'crazy but a great surprise'. This year's 32-man long-list was drawn up by one selected journalist from each UEFA member country voting for their best five players, and even a single nomination – believed

54

to be from the Welsh journalist who voted – was enough to earn Davies a place".

The Beeb had some more comments from Les. "I'm overwhelmed, flattered and honoured. There are so many emotions running through me at the moment. It's all just a bit mad. I know the journalist - he's done a good job with the Welsh Premier League over the last few years, I owe him at least a couple of drinks."

The North Wales football website *Bêl yn y Gogledd* (Ball in the North) had more to add. "The fact that a player from North Wales' Bangor City was being talked about in the same conversation as Lionel Messi and Cristiano Ronaldo truly caught the imagination of the whole UK."

Sadly, Les was later pipped to the award by Andres Iniesta. Apparently, Iniesta is also good but he doesn't play for us. Dave Jones admitted that although the Truck wasn't his first choice, the recognition for his outstanding contribution to the top flight of Welsh football was deserved. "When I was the Welsh media judge for UEFA's Best Player in Europe contest in 2012, I didn't choose Les as one of my five top players for a joke. I felt the way he had been so dominant in the Welsh Premier in the previous season was deserved of wider coverage."

I'll have to be more polite to Les the Truck, from now on.

A home game for Bangor v Mynydd Llandegai

Mynydd Llandegai is a small quarry village on the edge of Snowdonia and hosts an enthusiastic local team from whom we pinched their centre forward earlier in the season. Both teams took a break over Easter and met on 19th April.

I was promoted to physio due to the lack of our existing two physios. I had planned to get my kit bag filled from the cupboard in the stock room but the task was made more urgent as I had to tend to sore ankles and backs before the game. I discovered that the keeper of the keys for the cupboard was usually Chris the coach. He lent them to me and a quick pillage of the stock room followed, after a brisk jog from the sore ankles and backs in the changing rooms, toward the pitch which is next door to where the stockroom lives. I then filled my monster sized physio bag with what I could. I had taken so much that I felt as if I was lugging around a body in it but, undaunted, I proceeded to lollop back as best I could to our changing room once again. Before the team left for the game, Johno asked if any players needed further treatment. They took a look at me, seeing that I was neither Rhys nor Trudy, they decided that they were as good as they could be and set off to deal with Llandegai.

This was an evening game with a beautiful backdrop of the Britannia Bridge, a modified tubular railway bridge designed by no less than Robert Stephenson himself, originally carrying the Holyhead to London mainline railway. It was later modified after a fire destroyed the tubes and now carries the A5 and the railway; one above the other across two majestic arches. This links Anglesey to the mainland as an addition to the older Menai Bridge further east along the strait, which is not visible from our ground. Anyhow, the point was that the evening sun was sinking toward the silhouette of the Britannia Bridge and toward the surrounding trees producing a striking but, I must admit, a blinding backdrop to the west side of the pitch. Our floodlights gamely tried to even out the light imbalance but on this occasion were overwhelmed by Mother Nature. Until half time, the sun seemed to bleach most people's view apart from some fans on the west side of the ground with their backs to the sun who were able to see roughly what was going on. The dugouts are on the opposite side and all their occupants were at best partially sighted.

Llandegai were comfortably nestling midtable and surely ideal opposition for us chasing the title. So it proved. But to begin with, a smart forward lofted pass from the Llandegai midfield set up the tempo of the game with the opposition playing most of the attractive footy in the first half. Their forward looked to beat our offside trap on the right wing but then trod on the ball and fell over. He then rolled about as the ball squirmed off for a throw to us. The ref considered stopping the game as the footballer was on the floor and I presume a severe head injury was suspected. With characteristic lucidity, Johno read the situation as did the ref.

"Hey ref – that player's not injured, he's just embarrassed."

Play continued.

The Llandegai goalie saved a penalty, blocked several shots but still had a busy time picking the ball from the back of the net. To top it all Dylan Williams (Dyl Bach or little Dyl our midfielder, not our previous team manager, big Dyl) remodelled a Cruyff turn by letting the ball bounce over his head after dummying a defensive run back to his own defence to turn on two of the opposition and lead a charge to Mynydd Llandegai's goal. The Dyl Bach double flick. Class. No goal followed but that was what such a delicious flick deserved.

A header from Corey Jones opened the scoring for the Blues on 11 minutes and seven more followed before Tomos Williams from Llandegai looped one over Cian, our goalie with the last kick of the game. 8-1 and we took the fight to Boded who did not play that evening.

Wisdom always emanates from our dugout

We all know that footballers are incapable of making decisions without our constant help as fans, coaches or as match officials. Most decisions have to be made in milliseconds and so most are instinctive, but advice we give. Endlessly. And our bench is just as helpful. Johno is allowed to constantly encourage, enrage and enrich, but the rest of us like to help like a chorus line in a musical. The subs are sat on the bench usually being pretty quiet. Rhys and I are hanging around together with a variable combination of the rest of the management team of Mel, Merv, Gareth (Gaz), Chris and Aled. Together we make quite a racket. Usually six or seven of us are stood up which has often caused some criticism from any obstinate ref who may permit only two, that is Johno and one other, to stand. So, we sit for a while and before long we are on our feet once again, throwing our collective toys out of the pram. Generally, the ire is directed to the oppo's bench over the most menial of indiscretions. Usually debatable fouls and offsides are a favourite to produce polar opposite views of the truth from both of the benches. Players' inability to find space, hang back or push forward are other moments of crises. Sometimes the most minor conflict of opinions, or behaviours, can be an excuse to fire off and then I would cower at the back of the dugout. Players would poke out their chests and have a meeting like dodgems in a fairground with more responsible do-gooder players trying to separate both sides of any so-called 'debate'. Usually unrepeatable expletives are exchanged rather than dinner dates before the referee gives an arbitrary judgement. Our large entourage of support means that the crowd is predominantly 1876 in any game and so usually sides with whatever our dugout is complaining about. Within moments it would all stop just like hissing cats. After the game we would all be the best of mates.

Mel as club manager has managed the first team as well as Johno, the team manager, and during games they frequently exchange words, Mel with arms folded, is reflective and quietly offers suggestions in Johno's ear. Incidentally, Mel works as an Occupational Therapist in mental health and the current team sponsors kindly provided financial support for local deprived children and mental health services via his link to football. Returning to the dugout, Johno will resolve matters by shouting louder than any-one else and provides an excellent, if not biased, ongoing commentary of the game.

Merv is the goalkeeper coach and I have only ever heard fluent French slung from his mental kit bag to the general effect that we are totally crap. Still there is sensible advice to be had. He works for Border Force so I think our land borders are safe, particularly at Holyhead where he works. Then we have three first team coaches. Gaz is the quiet one and stands tall above the rest of us, big framed glasses like Harry Palmer, unshaven, as visible as a lighthouse, studying, assessing, formulating and then about once or twice a game explodes like a neutron bomb. Within 15 seconds he returns to his reflective state, slowly re-arming. I think he works for the KGB. Rarely speaks. Arms folded. But he smiles and is polite. Studying, assessing, formulating. Always. You are never entirely sure whether or not he may be keeping mental notes as evidence against you, and your family may disappear at any moment. He tells me he works for a bank, but he would if he really works for the KGB. Chris has an interest in junior training and of course is the hallowed keeper of the stockroom keys. He reminds me of a pet Labrador puppy. Small, impossible to offend, always bouncing around with suggestions and full of devilish fun. He barks at all the passers-by, eats your slippers and poos in all the wrong places (I confess I have no evidence of the last point). He just wants to be taken for a walk. Aled is a graduate of the University Campus of Football Business, based at the Mecca of football, the Etihad Stadium in Manchester. In his day job he works for FIFA and his line manager is none other than the ex-Arsenal boss Arsene Wenger. Of course. Fortunately for Aled, I regularly advise him about team tactics and about the offside rule. Aled is very polite. There is no industrial language from him which I find refreshing and he pretends that he is learning something from me. Then he walks to the far end of the dugout and continues to study the game that I am supposed to be watching. It turns out that he is a professional assessor of team strategies and tactics which he reports to FIFA but I found this out only after several months of me providing him with what I considered to be sound advice but which, of course, was entirely useless rubbish. Aled is walking up Kilimanjaro because he is extremely fit but he also has a cause. It is to raise money for the mental health charity 'Mind' after the tragic death of a friend due to mental health problems.

I am not sure why we have such a large retinue of team managers and coaching staff at each game as we usually have at least twice as many staff as our opponents. Maybe our results across the season justify such attendance. Nonetheless, amongst this menagerie our team has to make sense of comments flung at them and turn them into balletic moments of joy several times in every game.

Johno gets on well with Mel, Merv, Gaz, Chris and Aled who all pull in the same direction. I have made them sound a bit like Dave Dee, Dozy, Beaky, Mick and Tich, the off-piste rock band from the 1960s but any similarity between the two sets of performers probably stops there. Away from the music, team selection is a group effort with no hierarchy in decision making. Having said that, final team selection is up to Mel and Johno. All players and management work as one to be demonstrative on the pitch and to offer support to each other, when needed.

Well done lads.

The penalty shoot-out

I was often told in medical education that piss poor preparation makes for poor performance. The five p's to get it right. I guess the same is true in sport with training being a core part of the schedule that also includes competitive games and friendlies. The cohesion of the team is paramount and is improved with training so that every-one understands their roles during a game. Thanks to adequate pre-match preparation all players should be fit enough to run around for the duration of any football game too. That includes any extra-time.

I have attended a few training sessions when neither Rhys nor Trudy were available but nothing prepared me for how the session was to finish on one particular summer's evening at Treborth.

During this relatively jovial low intensity training stint, I had a quiet time with no injuries to sort so Johno got me involved with umpiring a game of keepy-uppy volleyball between the lads. He felt sorry for me looking a bit lonely in the dugout. Being an umpire turned out to be fun taking on the mantle of the ref, inevitably making decisions that didn't please at least one half of the trainees. This particular exercise is the same as volleyball but without hands, controlling the ball with anything but. It was all good fun and I contributed by making more than my fair share of random decisions due to my selective deafness and selective blindness. Then followed a game of five-a-side and at the end of the session, I started to tidy up some of the pitch markers and small nets we used for both the volleyball and five-a-aside.

Then there was an interesting development which caught my eye. One of the five-a-side teams moved to the goal line of a full-size goal net; bent over with their backs to the pitch and lowered their shorts before the other team started taking a penalty each aiming for the five exposed backsides. I looked uneasily around to see if there were any passers-by that might be witness to this strange ritual but the training ground was otherwise deserted so late in the evening. I let out a sigh of relief. There was a lot of giggling and I wondered if I was witness to some sort of sporting initiation to a pagan order of 1876. Needless to say, none of the penalty takers missed the nets. Three hit their intended targets with what I must say were excellent penalties with two hitting the right cheeks and one the left of two of the five mooning players with one particularly unlucky participant being hit in the butt twice. None of this Panenka rubbish. My description of the impact sites may be slightly inaccurate as I ensured I was a good distance away in case the police arrived. Even from where I stood, each direct hit looked painful to watch as the stricken players fell over like ducks at a shooting gallery and bemoaning their bad luck. This generated even more hilarity and I remained mesmerized with what was going on. They slowly got back to their feet, only to resume this rather gruesome series of moonshots that outshot NASA. The penalty takers showed great resolve and professionalism to see the job done.

Afterwards all returned to the dugout. I was bemused by all of this and later I asked Johno what was the reason for this apparent sado-masochistic activity involving him and four of his teammates being shot at. He said that his team lost the five-a-side. Fair point.

As the two moonstruck players gingerly sat down to change their clothes at the end of the session, Johno launched into a de-brief and plan for the next match. There were none of the usual injuries so after Johno's chat I asked if any-one wanted bottom cream. The two sad and bad-ass people looked as if they had six of the best from their headmaster. I certainly wasn't offering to rub it in. There were no takers.

Bangor v Nefyn United

St George's day has little importance in North West Wales especially as St George did it for one of Dave the Dragon's mates. But it was the day we played Nefyn, a team from a beautiful coastal town on the north side of the Llŷn Peninsula. Somehow, by magical forces and like at Bodedern, it had created 11 hardy young men who had crafted their way to fifth place in our league. Nefyn were one of the few teams that took points from Bangor in a difficult away game in January that ended in a 2-2 draw. We expected a hard game. It was hard in several ways. We quickly conceded a goal with Nefyn's first attack. Then they proceeded to hack our players down at every opportunity and in keeping the ref busy, his poor yellow card looked a little frayed at the edges before too long.

Johno claimed he had witnessed a miracle and announced it as so to the indifferent ref when one of the Nefyn's midfielders fell in a heap on their left wing only for him to jump to his feet moments later, unaided, Lazarus-like as Nefyn saw no point in delaying their subsequent free kick. Johno was also unhappy when one of our team made a half-hearted challenge.

"Hey, does he owe you money or summut? Tackle him like you mean it mate."

We had drawn level with a spectacular penalty scored at the third attempt after two parries from their luckless goalie before our midfielder Cam Barry squirmed the ball under the keeper and into the net. The inevitable happened when one of their defenders collected a frayed yellow too many and was shown red and the man advantage that followed for us turned out to be too much for Nefyn to withstand. We were already ahead before the man advantage was able to come our way.

As the physio for the day I found plenty to do for various minor ailments yet the ref was busier, repeatedly sorting out pitched battles between opposing players. The second busiest on the pitch was Nefyn's goalie in contributing to assists for our team goals and other artistic but ineffectual balletic leaps in what turned out to be an 8-2 thrashing delivered by our boys still applying the pressure on league leaders Bodedern Athletic. Corrig was on fire and bagged four goals that day. He arguably should have been man of the match but in my mind the Nefyn goalie won the day. His dramatic skills should have won him an Oscar as well. There was more hopeful news in that Boded were pegged back 1-1 deep into the second half, away to fourth placed Penrhyndeudraeth, a capable team that held us to a goalless draw early in the season. Penrhyndeudraeth is difficult to find and almost as difficult to say (pronounced pen-rin-day-drithe). It is a small town nestling just around the corner from Porthmadog just beyond the reach of Snowdonia, sandwiched between the quaint Ffestiniog and Wales Highland Railway and the river Dwyryd. Most occupants of our dugout had their Cymru Football Apps open, constantly checking the Boded latest score and for some reason not reflecting on how beautiful Penrhyn was. Boded kept us waiting but just like all great winning teams were not fazed by their apparent predicament: hammering home their winner with 15 minutes remaining. Boded still had a five-point lead over us going into the final three games.

Our changing room

If you happen to stray into our changing room when the gang are preparing for a game it just looks like the sort of bedlam you would expect in a child's bedroom. It is all set up nice and tidy by an invisible pixie before all becomes outrageously noisy and turned upside down by its rowdy occupants. I usually arrive when players return from their warm up and so the changing room is already a tip.

There are multiple calls of "Hi Doc" from around the boys. A small amount of gossip is exchanged but most opinions surround the ensuing game, the opposition, the strengths and weaknesses of their team and to a lesser extent the performance of the boys in our previous game. Les, Shaun and Johno usually lead the squabbling. Defender Joe Culshaw (Cully) cuts in with training issues. Injuries are discussed but before long Tom's music system is launched into action and then no one can hear anything save the intense thudding of rave music. Occasionally there is some Dad music which I may have a sporting chance of recognising, such as an Oasis song I was able to bop along to in an attempt to join the party. Almost always the latest dance tunes are thrashed out. Shortly my head is pounding and I try to concentrate on any injuries or strains that need sorting. There is an overwhelming smell of Deep Freeze and Deep Heat added to with the occasional eau de burp and farts.

The changing rooms at Treborth were decorated mid-season, and somehow it seems a little smaller. Since we returned, the massage couch lost its usual place at one end of the room. So, no easy place to provide massages and also nowhere for me to sit to soak in the environment as that was my chair when not otherwise occupied. One week it turned up in the shower and at other times it ventured quite a distance to the stockroom by the pitch. The poor couch needs a permanent place of its own. Then the coaching talks begin which means Tom's music is silenced. Thankfully. Johno, Mel, sometimes Gareth and rarely Merv speak. We all listen, the more senior players add a few words and mutual cheering and back slapping follows. After high fives, whoops and other random encouragement, in single file the players clop towards the pitch for the game.

Half time sees an update from Johno or Mel with a debrief from the first half, usually encouraging and tweaking strategy to improve matters ahead of full time. Performance is relentlessly reviewed and if not perfection, why this is not so and who needs to change what they were doing to rectify matters. I recall Johno scalding the boys on one occasion, for being only 4-0 up at half time. I thought he was joking but I soon realised that he wasn't. It was the performance; not the score. Any injuries are reviewed at that point.

At full time the mood totally depends upon the result. So far this has usually been upbeat. Tom is back on the diva tunes and then a sight that should stay in the changing room with various nudes back slapping each other and dancing around on their various circuitous routes to the shower. I avert my eyes from this harrowing scene. A large pile of dirty kits seems to appear all by itself in the middle of the room.

Once I asked Tom if he could improve his ghastly taste in music and with his usual laid-back but helpful attitude he obliged.

"Sure, what would you like?"

I was confused and put on the spot by his apparent interest. In my panic I blurted out the first thing that entered my tiny skull.

"Heavy metal please."

"That's a done deal, Doc."

I can take about two or three tracks of heavy metal before my brain screams for a quieter life so I don't know why I said that. If the rock'n roll rocks I will have to pretend that I am enjoying it. Me and my big mouth.

Before everybody packs up to go their own ways, there is a final team talk, looking at the positives and negatives and what is scheduled for the week ahead. That usually involves a two-hour practice session at Treborth midweek and a game at the week-end. Finally, the players collect their boots and the coaches collect up all kits to be taken away for washing prior to the next match.

All players understand that home or away the changing rooms are provided for our benefit and must be left in the same condition that they found them at the outset by the invisible changing room pixie. So, in reality the boys are not children but responsible and proud members of our local community.

A sports psychologist

There are always reasons to have psychology in sport. We use kidology all the time to convince ourselves we can do couch-to-5k and not kill ourselves, to push ourselves harder or even to get out of our beds when really, we would rather not. This is self-motivation and without it nothing would get done. We would still be living in caves waiting for someone to invent fire or design a wheel or at least buy some central heating.

Does a football team in the fourth tier of Welsh football need to get serious about sports psychology? Well, we do need to know what it involves. There are two aspects to sports psychology. The first is how sport can improve general wellbeing with lowered stress and an improved mood. This is called clinical sports psychology. The second is how performance can be enhanced with an improved psychological approach which is called educational sports psychology.

The issue of mental health in sport has been touched upon with the work of Abbey Road and with Aled climbing Kilimanjaro to raise funds to support mental health. Mutual support is already available within the team. Contrary to the saying there are no I's in team: each team is full of I's. Each with his, or her, own reasons to participate. Togetherness, engendered by a team ethos adds a common purpose, a routine and with it, responsibilities. The penalty shoot-out at the end of one of our training sessions is a further example of a mutual bonding that can be encouraged between colleagues. Work outings, such as whitewater rafting, a group walk, a meal or a trip to the pub would have similar intentions. If necessary, more professional targeted help can be made available for those with more challenging mental health problems and clinical sports psychology can achieve this need in a sporting environment. Mutual support can be offered by all and that should be advertised by the coaches and by me. Sports psychologist and mental health team support should be offered for problems that are not resolved easily or unlikely to be resolved in-team by peers.

Educational sports psychology uses relaxational techniques: stopping negative self-talk and substituting less negative with more positive outcomes and using motivational goal setting with SMART criteria which are also clear, challenging, reflective and committed. This is a more structured motivational approach I mentioned earlier. There must be time to complete complex tasks. SMART is an acronym for specific, measurable, appropriate, reasonable and timely. There should be specific goals; measurable outcomes of attainment; appropriate goal setting relevant to the individual and team objectives; such goals must be reasonable in that the expectation is that outcomes are attainable; and that these must be timely so that a date of completion is useful to the individual. SMART criteria include developing motivation, willingness and willpower to achieve agreed goals.

Routine sports psychology to improve outcomes remains aspirational for Bangor 1876 at present. This is offered in a lay sense already by the team managers and coaching staff, mostly instinctively, with every training session and on matchdays, and requires us having to know how our players function considering three influences: of the player, the constraint and the environment. This could be objectivised using an introvert-extrovert assessment. There is no plan to instigate professional sports psychologists into routine training yet, although one team manager and one coach have degrees which have sports psychology as part of their curricula, a third who is currently a player has a sports psychology master's degree. We intend to draw upon their experience for future seasons. Aled is one of the three and is happy to work with me to offer educational sports psychology with motivational and relaxation techniques. The details of who does what are being developed. This should be fun as neither of us has done this sort of thing before. Hopefully we won't trash the brains of our first team.

Finally, links will be explored with Bangor University School of Sport, Health and Exercise Science.

The teas team, Bar Uno and 1876 in the community

The café in the clubhouse is the nucleus of Bangor 1876. The team of Linda, Mandy, Dylan Reggae and his daughter Frida exemplify the friendly nature of the club. Dylan's other daughter, Megan also helps out occasionally. Their highly appreciated task has been to serve coffee, tea and beer and other goodies pre-match as well as at half time with great cheer so keeping the Bangor faithful full of high spirits (sometimes literally) and so indirectly supporting the team in their actions on the pitch. On the developmental front, I gather that an 1876 beer and a Mona Lager are planned. Forget men walking on the moon, 1876 branded beers and lagers are definite giant leaps for mankind. Week in and week out the teas team is dependably serving us in our hours of need. They also give me a free coffee every home game for which I am internally grateful.

Linda and Mandy migrated from Bangor City where they had helped out for years selling programmes, working the turnstile and serving teas. They were both delighted to move across to 1876 to help out in the café and also to see games.

Dylan Reggae loves reggae music, as his name clearly suggests, and occasionally is a DJ purely playing reggae. He has a striking appearance as he is tall, slim and possesses a deeply tanned skin of a person who enjoys the great outdoors. He usually sports a brightly coloured Rasta beanie hat. His face is permanently decorated with a broad grin complemented with an engaging gaze. When asked why he helps in the café, Dylan admitted selflessly that someone has to do it. He acknowledges that all 1876 staff are unpaid and all have to muck in to provide the many day-to-day chores needed for any football club.

Dylan is an eloquent speaker and has been forthright with his views about the recent downfall and mismanagement of Bangor City. Working on behalf of the Bangor City Supporters Association, Dylan Reggae worked in City's café and he became more discontented with watching the football, as well as the off-field antics with his former team. Catering appeared more enjoyable. Continuing this with 1876 seemed a natural progression. He felt that this was not too demanding, the environment was relaxed and friendly and he was supported by the rest of the teas team. As there are less people to serve than at Bangor City, Dylan has found it easier to follow the football with 1876, which he appreciates more these days, once he has served fans at half time. As he doesn't have to be a part of the teas team at away games, he gets to enjoy all the away football, first halves too.

He first got into reggae music when serving in the merchant navy in the Caribbean and became absorbed with the local culture and, naturally, the music. He met others with a common interest and set up his DJ hobby but also raised money for important causes including supporting striking miners in South Wales in the early 1980s. There were no specific influential musical artists, just those up and coming reggae acts particularly with a political narrative commenting on social injustice.

Always one to plough his own furrow, an artisan, socialist and a laid-back reggae dude who enjoys the local craic, this latter day *'Citizen Smith'* character hasn't lost his Hertfordshire accent undiluted by all his years in Wales. He seems interested in infiltrating Dafydd's mid-80s pregame

Dad-rock playlist with some left field choices of his own. His reggae leanings may also get a chance to be aired at more extended match day entertainment planned by the Comrades.

Dylan is a County Councillor for Gwynedd Council and is also a Councillor for the smaller Bangor City Council. His ward is in central Bangor. He supports the not-for-profit nature of 1876 as a community club, supported and run by its fan base. He has an interest in moving the ground to the old Bangor City ground at Nantporth. He stepped down from any neutral official capacity regarding this matter to provide his support on behalf of 1876.

Dylan's daughters work at a café in central Bangor called Bwyd Da (which means 'good meal' in Welsh). It is financially supported by the local Health Board in helping people recover from drug addiction and providing good quality food at low prices. The place looks like a nightclub on the outside but is a relaxing place to enjoy a tasty meal, a brew and a chat once on the inside. Dylan likes to go for a coffee and lunch.

James Deakin, another 1876 fan and moiderer 'marginal' (still more of that later), is the manager of Bwyd Da. James describes himself as the chief executive, bottle washer, toilet cleaner or let's face it the 'Mr Everything'. It is run by a charity called the North Wales Recovery Community dealing with homelessness, substance abuse and mental health problems. Bwyd Da helps people have a sense of belonging and helps them reintegrate into the local community as well as help remove long term barriers to employment. Drink related deaths have increased during the pandemic and Bwyd Da aims to identify problems at an early stage. 1876 works closely with Bwyd Da in its role as a community club providing a community initiative that aims to support individuals who have experienced mental health issues or addiction and this includes building links across a range of organisations. Like Abbey Road, Bwyd Da is another example of 1876 having indirect links with those providing support for the local community. Although a dyed-in-the-wool Manchester City fan, James was pleased to be involved with a club from the beginning and so feels a genuine loyalty to 1876.

Every game needs a debrief just like after every military op into enemy territory. Bar Uno provides the hospitality needed to feed the troops upon their return from combat following all home games. The links with Bangor University are emphasized with Bangor University not only owning the Treborth pitch but also Bar Uno approximately a mile away. Both the home and away teams and most volunteers, including me, pile into cars and head along the main road beside the Menai Strait. A free post-match feed is delivered with a mighty pile of steaming bangers and French fries for our hungry boys. Beer and lager also flow to assist the developing wisdom of the evening. This is not the warm down post game I had imagined for the team but that is a work in progress.

It was at Bar Uno that I discussed with Aled, and a supporter called Mash, the importance of cooling with ice baths after an injury. This would become a project to take forward to the following season with Bangor University. Aled thought that this was reasonable. When I spoke to Rhys and Trudy, they also thought that this was reasonable. Mash served in the Army and is used to the deprivations that go along with active service. He worked during, and after, his active service as a Humanitarian Land Mine Detection Dog Handler and searched for land mines. His knowledge of sports science appears genuinely academic and he has an interest in the therapeutic properties of cooling. We considered a practical solution that was affordable for 1876. Our local answer to Wim Hof was aware that a former Bangor City and Manchester United footballer called Clayton Blackmore used to dive into a wheelie bin full of iced water after games. It must have taken ages to fill. My concerns were that wheelie bins might be quite difficult to get out of, or that they may be tipped over with their precious cargo of iced water lost forever. Unless the user is extremely tall or is a contortionist, there is a possibility that the victim may not be able to get in, or once in, would not be able to get out. Despite these reservations the local University rugby teams are interested in post exercise muscle cooling and the University sports department is interested in getting at least one wheelie bin to be used exclusively as an ice bath. We would need to get a hose to connect to a local standpipe which can be done, but I presume that the used water would just need to be tipped out by pushing over the wheelie bin which sounds a bit calamitous. We can add some rubber ducks but we can also add at least a Happy Hot Tubs Daisy Duck Floating Thermometer and then we can scientifically check the water temperature all the way down to freezing point. I wouldn't like to be the last player using the ice bath, which would be warmed by numerous hot bodies, and by then the not-so-icey water would be swamp-coloured thanks to mud and various other bits of debris to add to its healing powers. I can foresee some potential health and safety issues here. No matter, these peripheral concerns can be brushed aside with more beer. Perhaps we could work on a smaller scale with buckets of iced water. Bar Uno helps us work on ideas like that.

Bangor away to Glantraeth

That is football. The phrase that says nothing but says it all: for you cannot be prepared to win if you cannot take a defeat. Our opponents and hosts on this particular Friday evening in late April were a team towards the west coast of Anglesey close to a town called Newborough. We were able to beat the mid table team 2-0 at our place earlier in the season. However, Glantraeth FC were not to be overawed by our visit. Although only a cluster of farm cottages exist at Glantraeth, the football club has an impressive list of past honours. We were outclassed and outplayed by Glantraeth from beginning to end. Maybe the bobbly pitch was to blame but that would be unkind. Maybe the loss of our evergreen centre forward, Les, enjoying an untimely honeymoon in Mexico was also something to do with it. He was unrepentant. Or perhaps it was just 'football' whatever that means. Efforts from H failed to send shimmers in the back of the Glantraeth net. 'H' is a useful abbreviation that quickly gets his attention but could be confusing if that guy from the dance group Steps is ever around and that other guy that no-one found in the TV programme *Line of Duty* also, rather surprisingly, happened to be in the crowd, watching on. Sioned also peppered the away goal but had similar bad luck. Their goalkeeper had an inspired game. Tom Clark also should have scored a hat-trick but contrived to miss a hat-full of goal scoring chances.

Then time stood still, the birds stopped singing, the cars fell silent and all was in slow motion as collective jaws dropped open from the travelling Bangor faithful when the winner came from a Glantraeth free kick just before 80 minutes to break all Bangor hearts. We lost 0-1.

Jonathan in his match report lamented: "Unfortunately it was not to be for Bangor 1876 as they could not muster an equaliser and went down to only their second league defeat of the season".

There was no alien invasion that day, we just weren't at our game. Not even the not-so-pagan powers of the Gorsedd stone circle near Siliwen Road could turn this one around. Despite the beautiful evening, it was a miserable day and a slow gloomy trip home.

Our defeat meant that Bodedern were champions and we were far enough above the remaining teams, regardless of all outstanding results to be league runners-up. *The Bangor Aye* reported that Bangor 1876 acknowledged Bodedern were champions and that we congratulated them on their success. Like you do when you don't really mean it.

*Bangor (with white shorts) away to Glantraeth. Sunny –
but not for us. Picture courtesy of Matt Johnson.*

Bangor 1876 had to reboot and plan for a possible second
season in the North Wales Coast West Football League
Premier Division, a name which really needs editing a bit I
think, but at least with Boded's promotion to greater
heights, we would be unlikely to have to deal with them in
the following season.

Dylan Reggae had other ideas. He felt that promotion to
the Ardal league despite our second place would provide a
more stimulating competition for the club with more teams
playing football to the level of 1876. We were a square peg
in a round hole throughout our second season in the current
division. We felt our dominant performances in the vast
majority of games provided a dilemma for the FAW: to see
if we merited a discretionary promotion to the Ardal league
despite not being champions. This can sometimes happen if
other teams in higher leagues cannot meet the requirements

to compete in those leagues and so choose to be voluntarily relegated, providing vacancies for runners-up teams.

Dream we may, but 1876 had to focus on a game three days later once again away, down the road towards the western side of Anglesey, to our friends in Pentraeth.

The referee

It is difficult to avoid all the clichés that apply to being a referee. I suppose referees are a bit like traffic wardens or prime ministers: known to all and liked by no-one. Unlike officiating in the highest echelons of the game where there is mutual support from linesmen, fourth officials and those dreaded three letters, VAR, the referee of the minor leagues is a hostage to fortune and cuts a lonely figure. To compensate, our referees have absolute power to be used absolutely. In our league, the linesmen are supplied as vigilantes from the two opposing teams and there is a fourth official only in the most important of games. VAR sits deep in the imaginations of the expert fans, all of whom freely advise the poor referee of the wisdom of their latest complete Horlicks of a decision. Of course, other hot drinks are available.

At the beginning of each game, the two teams emerge prepared for combat, accompanied by passionate shouting and singing from the crowd and then follows a strutting matador dressed in black, with no cape or hat but with the sombre expression of someone who knows that destiny rests entirely within his (they have all been men this season) unwavering gift. And woe betide anyone who tries to question that other-worldly power. Most of the decisions, on balance, made by these black harbingers of destiny are correct but a sufficient number appear random and are made purely to make the team managers and assistants explode at regular intervals. There are no TV replays and a slightly loud and unrepeatable comment from anyone, anywhere can be heard by all when the total attending is usually no more than 400 albeit baying for blood. Decisions by referees are final, just as a Roman emperor deciding the fate of a gladiatorial combat, totally unquestionable and there is no appeal. I find the most amazing thing is that after 90 plus minutes of outrage there is almost instant return to collective decorum around the ground once more, the referee collects his fee, a respectable £30 per game not forgetting additional travel expenses, gets into his car and returns home happy that he has completed a job done well.

There must be a celestial calling to this ambassadorial role akin to being sent to the West Bank. No one thanks the referee who is the recipient of unrelenting verbal abuse from all quarters, yet they all seem to enjoy their marshalling role and come back for more opprobrium the following week. I don't think that I could handle that. Let us not forget that without our embattled refs we would have no competitive football, or 1876, and so they deserve our gratitude and respect at the end of the day. All referees are supported from the grassroots upwards by the FAW and The Referees' Association. Come back, for almost all is forgiven.

Yet – and of course I have a yet – there is a stand out figure worthy of a special mention who shall remain nameless. Sadly. This hanging judge is short with spiky hair who has terminal short man syndrome perfectly complemented with a prickly personality. If he turns up at the game you know you are in for a tough time. They say sport is a great leveller and so is this ref as the outcome would be entirely unpredictable, solely within his gift and nothing to do with the skill of the individual teams.

Decisions made on pitch are reliably random and there is an immediate loss of control of any game from each and every kick-off. His plum coloured overworked bugler's cheeks would abuse his poor whistle time and again. Yellow cards, red cards or any combination thereof would come flying out of his pockets at regular intervals until his pencil would go blunt and he would have to leave the pitch in search of a pencil sharpener. His shrill voice and abundant whistles would surely play out an overture to catastrophe every time. Players, the dugout and fans alike have no idea what is happening and hope in vain that the number of goals they see are the number that are officially recorded. I like to think that Bangor 1876 are not afraid of anyone in the North Wales Coast West Football League Premier Division but that is not true. We are fearful of this one particular ref.

Pentraeth v Bangor

May Day Bank Holiday Monday saw us away to strugglers Pentraeth who were 14th out of 15 teams in our league and the reverse of the first league game of the season. I must admit I have no idea what was missing three days earlier but despite conceding a goal, we scored eight, including another five from that T Rex goal scoring flame haired mini monster who signed early in the season from Conwy Borough, Corrig. Cully, H and Sioned also contributed to the scoring that day. Our great leader Johno was playing and must have got lost whilst wandering and accidentally headed an assist for the last goal of the afternoon for Corrig to press home. Bless Johno's cotton socks. That set us up nicely for the final game of the season on the following Saturday.

Jonathan was effusive in his praise for our new keeper: "Within a minute of the [our] opening goal, the hosts had a chance to get back on level terms when striker Kian Abbott found himself clean through on goal. However, Cian Thomas got out well to make the save. With just over 20 minutes left, Shaun Lock picked up a second yellow card and became only the second 1876 player to be sent off. Pentraeth sought to capitalise on their numerical advantage but Cian Thomas pulled off some excellent saves to repel their efforts."

*Goal! Bangor (with darker tops) back on winning form.
Picture courtesy of Dafydd Hughes.*

Perhaps this is as good a time as any to explain the Welsh football league structure as I understand it. I accept no responsibility for causing any confusion or headaches and I hope that you are sitting comfortably.

There are five tiers of leagues in Welsh football, tier one is the Cymru Premier League and is the only single league which covers the whole of Wales and is obviously where we should be. At the top. However, there are more than 100 clubs as well as the FAW who think differently. The subsequent leagues are divided on a regional basis. Tier two is divided into Cymru North and to Cymru South. Tier three has the Ardal (or district) leagues which are divided into the north and south leagues, each of which are divided in turn into east and west. Below the Ardal leagues are six Area Leagues which includes the succinctly named North Wales Coast West Football League Premier Division to which the mighty Bangor 1876 were promoted in the 2019/2020 season as unbeaten champions from the fifth and lowest tier called the North Wales Coast West Division One League. Needless to say, there are many leagues across Wales in the fifth tier. 1876 had to start in the lowest league when it was formed in 2019.

A small number of teams that are Welsh play in the English league and conversely a small number of English teams play in Wales. They all have their own reasons for appearing to play in the wrong leagues and the almighty and formerly named TNS from Oswestry is an example. So, now I hope that the Welsh League structure should be entirely clear for you. If so, then please explain it to me.

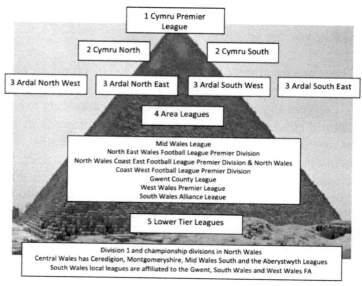

The 5 levels of the Welsh football league pyramid

The Moiderers' Corner

There is no strict English translation for the Welsh slang 'moiderer' but it roughly means rubbish, good times or bullshit. But you get the drift of the sort of banter that may bumble along between any gang of friends during a football game.

The Bangor Aye, helpfully advises university students new to the fair city of the importance of a moider or to be a moiderer: "To Moider can either mean to talk rubbish, to go on and on about something relentlessly, or you can also have a Moider or chat with someone, for example, I saw my mate last night and we had a good 'Moider' whereas a 'Moiderer' is someone who has a tendency to always talk rubbish. You can also be 'Moidered' by someone, for example someone on a night out who won't leave you alone."

Naturally during the realpolitik of a football season, the need to repeatedly moider requires a focal point for such important discussion. The Moiderer's Corner should be a location that you could find on Google Maps but for some reason it's not there. The position is variable during a game but follows a strict protocol. For example, at Treborth, for the first half the Moiderer's Corner is the corner near the corner flag where the players enter the pitch. Although I don't understand why, as far as I can recall we have always played from the Menai Strait end in the first half and so our location guarantees good close quarter views of first half Bangor attacks. Unfortunately, this is where I have to penetrate the group with my massive bag over my shoulder to get to our dugout. Every time I attract collective advisory and generally unhelpful comments from the moiderers. I flap my way through this fug of fake wisdom which doesn't really get me off to a good start.

Membership of this not so exclusive group includes Glynne, Les Pegler, let's call him 'Les money' to distinguish him from our esteemed centre forward Les 'The Truck' Davies, Rich, Rob and Robin who amongst his professional attributes is also an Ynys Môn (or Anglesey if you are not Welsh) County Councillor and so therefore is an expert moiderologist. All are long-time fans of Bangor City who became disenfranchised with the murky goings on before seeing a new way with 1876. All are 1876 Board Directors apart from Glynne who is Chairman of the Board. Les was the Chairman and Treasurer of the Bangor City Supporters Association and now deals with all the finances for 1876. Robin is an 1876 Board Director without portfolio: which means he has to do everything except for washing the kits and looking after the match officials which Rob has to do, and for dealing with the kit suppliers which Rich has to do. Rich is also an 1876 general dog's body. His words not mine. Overall as far as I can see, I think that leaves Robin with nothing. Rich seems to have a 'no portfolio' role as a general dog's body and so Rich and Robin both have the same no portfolio each and at the same time appear to do all the work so must have the biggest portfolios. I never understood management.

Rob kindly suggested that as a doctor I could be regarded as a pus-artist. As you can see, I do have quite advanced moidering tendencies but maybe I misheard or mis-moidered him. I must stress that there are several other club moiderers such as the Bangor Comrades, Dylan Reggae, James Deakin and others who expound the Celtic craft of moidering.

In the second half the moiderers congregate toward the opposite corner of the ground still following the 1876 left wing position, with the slightly naïve thinking that these locations will capture most of the action from our boys as they attack the opposition goal relentlessly during each and every game.

Now that you know where the moiderers lurk you can wisely avoid these locations to enjoy the excellent football to its full extent, relatively free of unwanted commentary.

Sioned sending in a bazooka of a cross in front of four of the most expert moiderers (from left to right, Rob, Les money, Rich and Glynne) before all four to a tee explode with verbiage of no value to any-one. Picture courtesy of Matt Johnson.

I like to think I am an ideas man. Usually good ideas. Les money is the only finance director I know (not that I know many) who has been booked by a referee for announcing his opinion of how a game was officiated, so with his fingers burnt he likes to keep clear of wise ideas and particularly he likes to keep clear of my suggestions. I don't wish to be indelicate here but Les does have form when it comes to breaking the law. He got himself a parking ticket whilst he was attending a Bangor 1876 Annual General Meeting. He was pleased that he received a 'discount' as he called it by paying the fine promptly until it was pointed out by a wiser moiderer (which doesn't narrow the field at all as he is the least wise of all moiderers) that this would be the full cost of the fine, not a discount and any later payments were indeed increased fines. I realised then that Les is not the person to go to trade any good ideas with as he has no common sense. There was a further twist to this story. Whilst Les was recalling his sad tale during a football game about how clever he was getting a bargain for his fine, I didn't realise that my car was parked illegally at this game and was awarded a parking ticket for my troubles. Which was paid promptly.

Then I thought that 1876 needed a nickname. How about the mountaineers? Rejected out of hand. 'Citizens' has been used from time to time but it doesn't seem to have stuck in common 1876 terminology. A mascot. Why as we keep on winning? We played Llandudno Town once and they had a mascot. It was none other than Dave the red dragon. We beat them 6-1. Let's concentrate on more important matters.

Returning to Les money's yellow card, this seemed to be a sensitive issue and a worthy subject to review. Les felt he was unfairly singled out after the ref concerned had finally had enough of the collective moidering fired at him and may have booked all the miscreants by wafting his yellow card in the general direction of several of the moiderers but with Les getting more of the waft than most. The identity of the ref remains confidential but I can confirm he was short with spiky hair. It was unclear exactly how many or if, indeed, any names were added to the yellow card that day, but legend has it that Les received the formal warning. After all, the ref can only book so many even if both sides of the card are used whether or not the ref's writing is incredibly small. But font size generally gets bigger when you are angry in my experience. The ref's squeals were so high pitched that only dogs and people with extremely sensitive ears could hear the Welsh reprimand which was presumed to be targeted at Les. He was lucky to get away with no pitch side ban or club fine and, in any event, I am sure the card has been wiped by now. Anyhow, the subject resurfaces in conversation quite frequently especially when Les is attempting to be pious.

I had yet more great suggestions. There was the intro music before each game so that our team could enter the arena at Treborth to a rousing anthem. I think I rejected this idea after some thought but starting in the fifth division of the Welsh League then *The Only Way Is Up* from Yazz and the Plastic Population seemed appropriate, or perhaps *The Final Countdown* by Europe would be an explosive rock and roll statement. Dafydd the Club Secretary, and supersonic supplies man, also turns out to be our musical maestro with a rich supply of electro pop and heavy metal for the pre-match warm up. Surprising for a man not in his first flush of youth, but he was certainly younger in the 1980s. I've done the maths and he would still be young for a Rolling Stone. He appreciated my suggestions. Treborth has a PA system to deliver uplifting musical standards pre-match but there is often no announcer and there is no PA during the football and so the crowd doesn't usually know the scorers and sometimes is ignorant of the score. There was a rumour that we won 15-1 once and it was hailed as a league record. Thank goodness for websites. Most of my ideas would have to wait.

Glynne wins for the idea of the millennium following a chat with a local publican who has agreed to rename a local beer 'The Moiderer' and the publican has kindly agreed to donate 30% of sales to 1876. Now why didn't I think of that?

Moiderer beer label. Courtesy of Glynne Roberts.

The final countdown with Bangor v Bodedern Athletic

Saturday, 7th May started with a chill but became warmer as the day wore on. I arrived early at Treborth to be greeted by the ticket staff. Les money and the ticket guy Cabs seemed pleased to see me.

"Hi Doc," Les piped up.

"Hi, I'm far too busy to speak to you guys today."

"Oh, why is that?"

"I have to keep the team shipshape."

"Oh no - is Rhys away, Doc?"

Cabs laughed

Aaagh. No respect around here! One of the team did want to borrow my scissors. Not exactly busy but no disasters caused by me. So far so good.

By the time of kick off at 2.30pm, Bangor 1876 was ready for a final flourish. Nearly 400 fans, including a noisy contingent from Bodedern, attended with anthems, taunts and the usual blue flares from the home fans to add to the occasion. We had fireworks too, on and off the pitch. Johno was certainly fired up. He warned our lads at the start that Bodedern had got to the last game of the season unbeaten and only drawing a game once. They figured that they were the 'Invincibles' already just like the famous Arsenal team of 2004 and their small but noisy contingent of fans sang that in high spirits. Johno was incensed, smoke coming from his nostrils and was more Dave-like than Dave the dragon.

"Right fellas, we focus on Boded now and stop all the shit about the invincible shit."

I have come across some pretty invincible shit in my time in medicine. It has never ended well.

"We give them a guard of honour but that is the only respect we give them, understand?"

Guard of honour led by Gareth (foreground left) and our boys for the Bodedern team.

We provided a guard of honour for Bodedern but as Johno demanded that was the only hospitality paid to them. Bodedern kept our defence busy especially in the first half and our goalie Ben Heald made skilful saves. This was an important game for both sides even though the league had been decided already. Our boys worked hard, quick passes and then moved into the spaces. Good pressing but no end product. Our heads didn't drop.

From behind the Boded goal on a slight embankment a small child, who looked as if he had been plucked from the film *Village of the Damned* with blond hair attempted to be cut into some sort of a hairstyle but ended up as a miniature blond version of Henry the Fifth, led a drunken adult crowd of (about four) rebel rousers describing how bad we were. Maybe they were Boded's version of the Jackson Five without the dance moves. Or the musical skills. Or the good looks. Or maybe they were further insurgents from the earlier alien landing at Bodedern. It was a little difficult to be sure from where I was standing, in the dugout near the halfway line.

The damned child shouted "who are shit?"

Rowsers replied quasi-musically: "Bangor".

The stirring next verse was more nuanced.

Rowsers "who are shit". In their defence the barber-not-quartet were quite co-ordinated which was an improvement on the Boded defence mostly in front of the goal posts.

Damned child riposte: "Bangor".

I was expecting the damned child to become Michael singing "ABC, it's easy as 123, as simple as do re mi..." with his henchmen spinning as one and the new Michael to throw in a moonwalk. Sadly, that didn't happen. He did appear a bit out of this world. But he was from Boded.

The Jacksons stopped their original score when successfully achieving a few encores after being met with total indifference from our lot and they became exhausted. Smoke from a blue 1876 flare drifted from the clubhouse and blotted them from view. Forever.

The football continued. Corrig opened the scoring after 10 minutes when a free kick from the right side of the box was played diagonally to the near post and he was there, as if by magic, to touch it past the keeper. Despite our domination a defensive lapse allowed Boded an equaliser just before half time. However, given the history between these two teams this was always going to be a fiery occasion and within a minute of scoring, their right back collected a second yellow following a fairly industrial felling of Corrig, just outside the Boded box. He was off and that probably changed the course of the fixture. Many possible fouls on our boys seemed to be waved away previously by the ref but Johno was pleased that the ref's right arm did work after all, and was able to haul his oh so heavy whistle to his mouth and blow for a foul in our favour. Bodedern were down to 10 men, but we still spooned the resulting free kick out of the ground.

Our coach, Labrador Chris, noted that one of the Boded coaching staff was vaping and that was against the FAW pitch-side rules. Chris proceeded to bark and yap whilst circling close to the linesman, close to our dugout as well as to the ref. The Boded coach hid his vape thingy and tried to say that the white vape smoke was coming from the recently let off blue flare. The ref bought it. The vaping stopped for about 10 minutes. Chris accepted his little victory and moved to concentrate on the on-pitch action.

After the break two goals followed for Bangor from Sioned and Corey Jones. The first was from a cross left to right and Sioned drilled a pacey shot low past the Boded keeper. The other followed a goalmouth scramble when one of our players was cut down with a likely penalty to follow, but the ref wisely saw an opportunity for an advantage to be played and before the defence could re-group, Corey (a defender by trade) was on hand to slam it home. Let it be noted that the ref made a second good decision that afternoon after the sending off.

Horror of horrors, I had to go on pitch to sort Cully's ankle after it got squished by a numpty from Boded. The ankle was painful to move so I moved it some more and yes it caused pain. No swelling, no blood. So far, so good.

Some Boded wisecrack from over my shoulder advised me: "you're not supposed to cause pain".
"Oh yes I am, I can make it worse and occasionally I can make it better."
I kept any further less polite thoughts to myself for once. Deep Freeze seemed to be the remedy. Do I spray the Deep Freeze over the sock or roll the sock down? Pressure. I

figured the fibre of the sock would chill enough if I blasted it without rolling the sock down or removing the boot. Phew. Cully got himself up and hobbled back into his left back position. He was OK. Johno was concerned.

"What was the problem?"

"Nothing serious, just a tiny hurty."

That seemed good enough.

Well, we ended their invincible hopes for the day, if not their already confirmed champions' status and their automatic promotion to tier three of the Welsh league pyramid, the Ardal League for the following season. At the end of the game, we finished with our heads held high and both sets of supporters drifted away from Treborth in good heart. However, a small number of Boded supporters managed to let their high spirits get the better of them when we accumulated for the debrief at Bar Uno and were then thrown out. Too bad. But how costly that earlier rain-soaked defeat away to Boded. Had we won that earlier game we would have been champions. No time for what-ifs in football. But time to plan for the new season ahead.

North Wales Coast West Football League Premier Division final standings		
1 - Bodedern Athletic	played 28 games	79 points
2 - Bangor 1876	played 28 games	74 points

All friends in the end. Mostly... Picture courtesy of Matt Johnson. Bangor in white shorts.

Jonathan added in his match report: "After the final whistle at today's game, a tankard was presented to 1876 fan Darren Thomas in recognition of his attendance at every game home and away this season. Our players, team managers, coaches, and officials are tremendously appreciative of the devotion and enthusiasm we see week in, week out from so many of our supporters. We would like to again take this opportunity to thank you all for the fantastic support at home and away in the league this season."

An obsession

The life of a football fan is never easy. It takes over your life; your family and your work are side-lined to the subs' bench and they rarely get a game. My thoughts, and passions are hidden away between games so that I can blend in with society and share ideals and dreams of normal people, but all too often an unguarded moment of casual conversation removes the lid to my Pandora's box of secrets and an outpouring of football micro-dissection ruinously overflows. I am not one of you: I am a football fan.

Pre-match rituals and post-match assessments are routine. An emotional roller-coaster of nightmares and happy places are commonplace. Supporting 1876, despite all of its current glory in its early life is just the same.

The start of the season, or the start of any match day, begins with high hopes; there will be no quarter given and at least the team is expected to put up a good show. Smash in many goals and re-write history. Demanded. But if not, then at least worry the opposition, keep them thinking and make them feel lucky that they may scramble something from the game. And so, we leave with our heads held high. That is the plan, but plans fall to bits, so said Mike Tyson, once you're punched in the mouth. This may be a painful truth as sometimes, however hard we try, our opponents just have all the answers. And the tide may inexplicably turn against us with a swathe of ridiculous decisions from an unpredictable ref and his two hideous myrmidons, the linesmen. But consider that just, and just sometimes we lose because we are not good enough. Maybe our defence was ill disciplined, too narrow, too far from the midfield or maybe the manager had the wrong plan. All to be discussed at the ensuing post-mortem at pubs, or other hostelries, immediately after any game. But excuses are legion and at the end of the day, we all live or die with the fate of our team. I think it is no more complicated than that.

Perhaps two or three days after a poor performance I can begin to return to how I was before, when I realise how the rest of the world has managed to cope, somehow, with this disaster and continues blithely as if nothing had gone wrong. I have no time machine and I cannot change fate. I attempt to fit into this new world, smiling with effort, pretending to listen with interest to others, and hoping I can once again function as a new me.

Yet win, lose or draw, there are always loads of important issues to discuss realising that it is not the taking part but the winning that counts. As far as I can see.

Opposing fans must feel the same pain and the same joy with their teams. I don't know and deep down I guess, to my discredit, I don't really care. Almost all seem pleasant enough people. Yet glory is always at the expense of others. Their songs are meaningless to us, their jabbing humour flat and not understandable. I think opposition grounds are not as welcoming as ours. Even their team kits are the wrong colours and of course not as pleasing as our own. Sometimes there are horror fashion shows with players forced to wear various gaudy creations much to the amusement of the crowds. Such cataclysms of colour must have a negative effect as shame-faced footballers attempt to display their silky skills yet be forced to dress like clowns. Goalkeepers so often seem to be content to display their peacock plumage of ridiculous kit. Perhaps the expectation is that the opposition would fall about laughing or be blinded as the teams with such stomach-churning appearances would win by 200 or so goals each game. No matter what tactics other teams employ, we outsmart them to take the three points and leave happy. At least that is the plan.

Our loyalty and passion for our club is unconditional yet I was surprised that I was able to develop a new allegiance not by desire but by circumstance. I didn't ask to be involved by 1876, it grabbed me. Perhaps the people I have met from the players, team managers, coaches, moiderers and others have all appealed to me as a community of like-minded believers preaching their ideals with a religious zeal to be on a common journey, and take the consequences, together, whatever they may be.

As far as I see it, you cannot choose your obsessions, as by fate they are chosen for you, serendipity or call it what you will but then you are locked in forever. As a football fan, I supported Manchester City because my father did and he put a picture of Colin Bell on my bedroom wall when I was a child. King Col was the first person I saw every morning staring at me when I woke up. Bangor 1876 was chosen for me because Glynne Roberts asked me to help and that was that. Allegiance is unflinching unless you take a brickbat too many and you walk away as if from any long-term relationship. I suspect that is what happened to the long-suffering fans of Bangor City. Maybe I have an addictive personality that, from time to time, flits from what I consider one amazing project to another, seemingly so important to me but not so to many of those around me. And maybe the religion of football is a good fit for my obsessive nature. I am not sure and perhaps it is easier for others to decide for me.

At the end of the day, glory is constantly aspired to whatever the outcome. Amen to that.

Season's end and then it wasn't

Dafydd was unable to slam Queen's iconic rock ballad *We are the champions* through his PA at the season's end. Alas, Queen never wrote the sequel 'We came second' but we cheered as if we had won anyhow. The invincibles turned out to be not so and we were happy for that, but in reality, we were taking crumbs from the king's table and that wasn't good enough. Coming second, is to be the first of the losers. At least to me it didn't seem that way. After all, our goal difference was the best in the league with 139 goals scored and only 19 conceded in 28 games. What a team!

But seemingly out of nowhere there were two cup competitions to finish. No-one was sure why there was a pile up of knock-out games to be completed. The first was grandly titled North Wales Coast Football League West Division Cup no less, involving clubs within our division in North West Wales. Fortunately, the name was shortened to the League Cup. What turned out to be a quarter final, the Friday following the final league game, was at home against a tricky Pwllheli team we beat twice in the league; but the first involved a winner in injury time.

We were playing on the evening of Friday 13th. Oh no, how many pairs of lucky underpants would I have to wear for this one? I haven't got any. I would have to designate some and have them anointed, or whatever you have to do to make them officially lucky. I needn't have panicked as on this occasion, by half time we were 6-0 up. We had so many goals that Johno was unsure of the score. By the end it was 9-0 with Pets having bagged four, Dyl Bach converting a penalty and both Corrig and Les Davies one each. Pwllheli added a goal of their own but this was in their own net. Geth got the last goal. So, the race to our boys' golden boot was between Les and Corrig and it was most definitely a remarkable contest. I calculated this as 28 each, but the moiderers' committee felt it was 30 for both Les and Corrig and so when Les was substituted in the second half I thought I would ask him.

"Haven't a clue Doc" was his answer. Not helpful.

Furthermore, there was a knee injury for a Pwllheli player who had to be substituted. There were none left and Chris Jones, our coach asked with a cheeky grin if I wanted to go on realising if I helped Pwllheli a 9-0 could easily become a 20-0 annihilation. Phew – I was not needed. That was close. A previously subbed Pwllheli player was permitted to re-start the game as we were winning by such a large margin. Not within the rules but not questioned. As expected, Johno was not impressed.

At the end of the game I passed Pets looking pleased with himself.
"Well done with the hat-trick Pets."
"But I got four!" replied Pets with an even bigger smile. Jonathan was purring in his post-match write up starting with "Bangor 1876 are through to the semi-finals of the League Cup after seeing off Pwllheli under the lights at Treborth". The rest of the report was a list of goals which was quite a read in itself.

Next up was Nefyn United; at home in the semi-final.

Saturday, 21st May was a beautiful late spring day fuelled with the anticipation that 1876 may get to a local cup final for the first time. The game was again at Treborth.

My day started well with Dafydd adding Europe's *The Final Countdown* to the music playlist to the lexicon 80s Dad rock I love. A lucky omen. I reckon we need at least three seasons before European football beckons and there are other priorities just now.

The game started with our boys setting about their business efficiently, quickly taking a two-goal lead thanks to an own goal and then a second from Geth. Nefyn pulled a goal back thanks to a deft free kick from just outside the penalty box with a ball that hit the crossbar and bounced into the net before spinning out. Shades of the England '66 World Cup final goal with that one, but the linesman immediately in front of our dugout said it bounced over the line. Fair enough.

Bizarrely, the strangest time-wasting episode from Nefyn followed, despite trailing the game and being awarded a corner, Nefyn's corner taker meandered to the relevant part of the ground where he showed no interest in the football but then proceeded to take a wee against the fence, as you do, with his back to the crowd. I stood just outside our dugout looking as bemused as the rest of those present at Treborth. I suppose that 'we time' is as important as 'me time' but the miscreant may have confused a 'we' with a 'wee time' as a cherished moment especially if spelling wasn't quite his thing. Fortunately, that corner of the freshly watered artificial turf was away from the amazed and deathly quiet audience. There was a collective sigh of relief when all realised that a number two was not required, and that play could continue. The ref chose to keep away from the offender. Justice was served when the resulting corner kick seemed to be lofted into outer space before it re-entered the Earth's atmosphere some time later, presumably descending at terminal velocity and now covered in ice, only to be dinked out of play some way from the goal off a Nefyn boot for a goal kick. The attacker who attempted to play the unplayable ice-ball-meteorite, may have had a sore neck staring into the heavens for such a long time and then a sore foot in attempting to kick what could have been a mass extinction event if the returning ball was allowed to strike the Earth. No booking for time wasting and no friendly advice from the ref for weeing in public.

Our goalie, Ben Heald was happy to resume normal service after this rather lengthy episode with Bangor still in the lead. Shortly after, we should have had a penalty and perhaps Nefyn's goalie should have been shown a straight red after a foul in the penalty box. Equally bizarrely, the ref gave a free kick to Nefyn and no cards. Our fans and our dugout were incensed. There was no pity from 1876 and a third goal from Corrig left us 3-1 up at half time.

Two more goals again from Geth and Corrig sealed Nefyn's fate in the second half with a 5-1 win for 1876.

Attackers from left to right Corey, Corrig, Les and a charging Tom preparing to receive a corner (all facing with no 'V' at the neck). Picture courtesy of Matt Johnson.

I was busy with Geth having been kicked and stamped on, H straining his hamstring and Dyl Bach with his long-standing low back pain which seemed to be a sacro-iliac strain. These were all dealt with plentiful Deep Freeze. Johno had to play in defence for the last few minutes as we had run out of subs after Tom was a casualty of friendly fire from our left back Cully who accidentally kicked him.

The rumour circulating around our team was that all games were to be completed by the end of May as the existing referees were paid only until then. That was to leave a possibility of four more games in the next nine days. Management of our players' injuries would be crucial to maximising the team's possibility of success. Rhys and I were suddenly in the thick of the action.

With great fanfare from all present that afternoon, 1876 were in their first final but next up, Pwllheli away in the semi-final of the other cup competition involving fourth tier clubs across the whole of North Wales, the Intermediate Cup. That game was scheduled for only three days later!

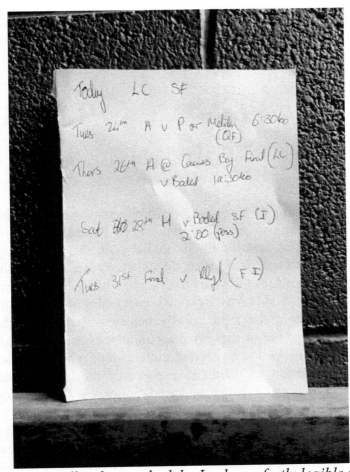

Johno's official cup schedule. Looks perfectly legible to me but I am a doctor. Picture courtesy of Michael Johnston.

As expected a game away to Pwllheli proved to be a tricky encounter. A 6.30pm start 30 miles from Bangor meant that several players arrived shortly before kick-off following the usual day-time commitments with no time for the warm-up. The weather had been fine for several days and a hard and bobbly pitch meant our ground game would also be unpredictable.

The evening of Tuesday 24th May was warm and sunny and the rolling green hills of the Llŷn Peninsula were at their beautiful best. Pwllheli sits between the picturesque town of Criccieth, with its castle and sandy beaches and the trendy Cheshire-set town of Abersoch, with its beaches, big houses and jet skis mowing down everything in sight; both in the water and on the nearby beaches. Pwllheli is the forgotten brother of these two iconic places and just needs a lot of love. Well to be honest, quite a lot of rebuilding too. It does boast a train link to the rest of the UK but that involves a tour of North and mid-Wales via Porthmadog and Barmouth, before twisting and turning inland to Newtown and Welshpool and then finally connecting to the rest of the rail network at Shrewsbury. Exhausting unless you are a train enthusiast. On a brighter note the Pwllheli FC coffers were swelled by the visiting faithful of 1876. On this occasion I gave Glynne a lift to the game. I forgot to bring my wallet so he had to pay my entrance fee. Again. Another beer would be repayment for a later date.

We found a grassy knoll, adjacent to, yet slightly raised above the pitch, and also where we were to be attacking in the first half so that we could fire some verbal pot shots at the oppo's defence. A good moiderers place to hang out. It turned out that most of the action was in our defence and we spent the first half squinting to get some idea what was happening, as we were a long way from the action.

The boys weren't at their best as passes were misplaced and players were out of position. Johno started the game. We had Sioned, Ben Owen in midfield and Alwyn Roberts (our newly signed centre forward) injured and unable to play. Corrig also could not attend. Tom did not wish to play fearful he may be injured before his wedding a few days later. He didn't want his wedding tackle tackled. I thought that was a reasonable excuse.

Before we knew it, we were 2-0 down with two long clearances to a speedy Pwllheli forward with excellent strikes to beat our defence and poor Ben Heald in goal. I was wisely advised by Glynne that we have never recovered from being 2-0 down. Were any of these offside? It was too difficult to tell from our grassy knoll and in any case the goals stood. By half time Pets managed to get a breakaway goal for 1876; he was playing well and attempted to lead the team by example. Surely, we cannot play another half as poor as that.

The second half continued in much the same way and before long, yet another big clearance from the Pwllheli keeper met the same striker to thunder a third against Ben. We were in trouble. That seemed to be the spark that woke our lot from the torpor that dogged them until now. We had time to re-group and play as a more co-ordinated team. Our better fitness was beginning to show. The game was pushed into the Pwllheli half, despite playing against the gentle wind and into the low evening sun. Goal line pressure ultimately resulted in a low close shot in from Dyl Bach and shortly after, an own goal for Bangor bringing the score level. The momentum surely was with us. But it happened again. A long goal kick, route one style that by-passed all

10 of our outfield players to the same striker onside, again, this time on the volley and spectacularly past Ben with 10 minutes to go. Unstoppable with a display of excellent ball control and an exceptional shot. Again, I was at the wrong end of the pitch and saw this momentous strike only from some distance. The locals ran onto the pitch convinced that the job was done. I must admit, I think that was the general feeling amongst the wilting visiting fans too.

Rhys was physio for the game which meant I was allowed to be a spectator but there were two head injuries for which I had to run onto the pitch, the second time I got stuck trying to clamber over the surround rail. On both occasions the players were able to continue. After all, they were in a better condition than my groin. I could and should have ducked underneath the rail. Note to self for the mental record, "please don't be a plonker and get injured whilst trying to get onto the pitch".

Returning to the more important events, Ben made a great save from a point-blank shot to tip over the bar. We were toast. But then, with Pwllheli tiring, they began to defend closer to their goal line and arguably with a touch of the gods themselves Corey Jones from the left side of the penalty box thundered an overhead kick into the far side of the oppos' net. That would have been impressive in the Champions League, never mind the North Wales Coast West Football League Premier Division. Four each and extra time.

This was not what we wanted prior to the Boded final two days later but beggars cannot be choosers. Pwllheli were struggling with fitness with several players going down with cramp. Bangor were now dictating the play and shortly before half time in extra time, Cully rifled in our fifth of the evening from a free kick 25 yards out to the left.

We had the lead for the first time in the game. The moiderers didn't know where to stand after so many changes of ends. Pwllheli had used all their subs and a player had to leave due to a hamstring injury. Another was sent off after a second yellow, fouling in frustration. There was no way back for the nine of Pwllheli who really fought hard all the way and indeed, Pets got a sixth shortly before full time with a pacey attack from the right, beating a defender with a rising shot. To misquote the great smoother than smooth soul god Barry White, Pet's scored the first, the last and he's our everything.

Pets on the run for his second goal of the evening. Picture courtesy of Dafydd Hughes

In a post-match reflection of the night before, Johno concluded that he needed a full body rub. That was definitely beyond my pay grade.

Our pitch at Treborth

3G or not 3G, that is the question. This was not quite what mad Prince Hamlet was contemplating when he was thinking of ending it all; but I think not 3G is the answer. We have the best pitch in the whole of the North Wales Coast West Football League Premier Division. Of all 15 of us. It is as flat as a billiard table. It is an all-weather pitch which means it is artificial and is green as green can be for plastic. The 3G or third generation synthetic design of the pitch has the correct pile height with a sand and rubber infill which is ideal for football. No mud or divots for 1876. It is more like a carpet than a lawn and under no circumstances should anyone be tempted to mow it. You have to wait a long while should the ball happen to bounce as it bounces high and injuries are more common with artificial pitches. As there is no soil that moves with twisting feet, boot studs can get caught in the mesh of artificial pitches causing ankle and knee sprains. Artificial pitches can also radiate heat on hot days and so water breaks should be considered more readily in these conditions.

We have visited grounds with slopes, that are rock hard and uneven or any combination thereof. In fairness, this is the sort of environment with which our boys are familiar. But the uneven pitches tend to limit our natural ground game and ironically a slope turns out to be something of a leveller against less skilled teams. As are mud and divots. The beautiful game of tiki-taka fast pass football promoted in the Spanish La Liga, and which we try our best to emulate, is replaced on bobbly pitches with a launch and chase tactic which seems at times a little unpredictable. We adapt pretty well to 'plan B' and we have to expect this tactical switch in many grounds in subsequent seasons.

Treborth has good pitch-side facilities including our licenced clubhouse and substantial changing rooms and so we cannot grumble. But we do. We have excellent floodlights permitting evening games as well as mid-afternoon starts which can be shrouded in gloom in mid-winter. I have suggested that Rhys shins up the stanchions and replaces a few dud light bulbs but as yet, without effect.

In the medium term, the team is keen to move from 3G to the conventional pitch at Nantporth previously used by Bangor City, almost two miles east of Treborth, again close to the Menai Strait; when our bank account permits us to do so. It has easy access to the main road unlike the long narrow driveway to Treborth and has a high-quality turf pitch. Turf means less injuries and so would please Rhys, Trudy and me, and please the players as well as all the fans. A win-win. And a few more wins. The larger ground capacity of 3000 at Nantporth may also give us an opportunity to expand our modest fan base. I hope that the main stand at Nantporth would be permitted to be named the 'Vera Owen Stand' if we were to move. Presently, we don't have an in-match PA nor, glory be, a scoreboard but if we were to ascend to higher leagues we may not score so many goals each game so perhaps then neither would be required. Maybe we would be better off remaining in ignorance until our phone Apps let us know the final scores a few hours later. That said, Treborth has been a marvellous facility for us as the perfect platform to display our fast ground-ball game and help us progress through the minor Welsh leagues.

There is a high surround fence around Treborth and we are all grateful for that. We are guilty of testing that fence, probably more so than opposing teams considering the large number of goals we have scored and the even larger number of shots that have missed their intended target. We have lots of footballs. We do need them.

I have acquired the essential ball boy skill of handing the ball back quickly to our boys for our throw-ins and oh so slowly to the away team when a ball has been kicked out to touch to where I happen to be standing. Unless we are not winning. I made a mistake to try to catch a ball once away at Blaenau Ffestiniog and managed to bruise my thumb. I realised then that footballs are as hard as bowling balls and my thumb was sore for weeks. Doctor heal thyself eh? I haven't tried to catch a ball since.

Then there are the wayward shots as well as various clearances that are blasted over the surround fence. Those familiar with our local geography will know that the Menai Strait lurks at one end of the ground and a number of wild shots clear the fence at that end, some of which clear the row of trees next to the fence and these balls are never seen again. In truth only the wildest of shots would get anywhere near the straits as there is a further field beyond the row of trees before the water. But I suppose it is possible that as the prevailing tide sees fit, balls could be carried out toward Caernarfon to the west or Beaumaris to the east. The solution to the problem has been accepted that our boys are to aim a little lower to save us a lot of money in lost footballs, score more goals and protect the local fishermen, and I suppose the fish from an occasional aerial bombardment. Hopefully Prince Hamlet would be pleased with this plan.

The League Cup Final

A mere 48 hours after the previous battle, the walking wounded returned, again for an evening game, but this time for our first ever cup final. After two years of Bangor 1876 being in business we were to slug it out with none other than, of course, Boded for the chance to collect our first ever honour at the League Cup Final.

Memories of James Bond meeting his evil genius nemesis yet again for a climactic showdown spring to mind. Our intrepid operative has been captured and escorted to Boded's secret lair by two henchmen almost as evil as Dr Boded himself, but obviously a bit more stupid and so will not do well in the long run. Dr Boded is sitting on his executive high back swivelling office chair (£115.99) lovingly stroking his favourite Adidas FIFA World Cup 2022 Al Rihla Pro Football in front of a huge collection of stuffed referees. The short ref with the spiky hair is missing from this ghoulish collection and indeed this maybe because he is a member of SPECTRE and still active doing his devilish worst. Membership of the covert criminal organisation must explain this ref's unpredictable behaviour and we may need to know how to neutralise him next season.

"So pleased to meet you 001876."

"Dr Boded – the pleasure is all mine."

First team coach, Gaz from the KGB would fulfil the Roger Moore character quite nicely. Perhaps Gaz is really with MI6. He must obviously escape this fateful meeting only to fight it out at the ultimate dénouement. I could just imagine Williams, Gareth Williams from a scene stolen from the film *Live and Let Die* with him standing pitch side as a study in calmness personified. But danger lurks and without hesitation he swivels backwards, whilst somehow lighting his Hai Karate aftershave which for some reason he happens to have about his person with a preposterously huge Cuban cigar, which for some reason he happens also to be smoking, I accept illegally, by the touchline but we'll skip that technicality; to convert his babe magnet aftershave into a flamethrower. After giving this some thought, I suspect that the bottle of aftershave, if it were to ignite at all, would act more like a hand grenade and blow our hero to smithereens but we can ignore that small potential risk. So, returning to the action: the flame throwing aftershave torches what looks like a pathetically unrealistic looking large plastic snake lurking in the undergrowth behind him leaving everything else unscathed. Job done, Gaz returns calmly to smoking his monstrous cigar whilst re-assessing the football game. Not a bead of sweat upon his brow. Young ladies swoon.

That thought made me feel a bit light-headed too. The evil Dr Boded had better watch out...

Daydreaming aside, there was a cup final to be had. The cup was confined to those in our league. As it happened the knock-out cup competition had followed the form of the league although this isn't often the case, but Boded and 1876 were the two standout teams competing for top honours. The site for this eagerly anticipated maelstrom was to be none other than the Twin Towers of Anglesey, the ground of Cemaes Bay currently in the North Wales

114

Coast West Football League Division One (which was one league below us) nestling between the sea and the rolling low hills of the north eastern part of Anglesey. Helpfully, for location purposes, Cemeas has Wylfa nuclear power station as a next-door neighbour which had been made eco-friendly as it was decommissioned several years ago.

The evening game followed one of the two days per week I remain in gainful employment at the hospital in Bangor. Getting to the game seemed simple in theory. Less so in practice. The clearly agreed arrangement was for me to be picked up after work from the hospital main entrance. Glynne was in charge of proceedings and was planning to drive me to the game. As it happened, I finished my day's work in good time and I headed for my car in the car park to exchange my work stuff for my mega-bag and an additional rucksack with food and other essentials. It so happens that the car park at the hospital is between the main entrance to the hospital and the roundabout at the front where cars can approach the hospital site. I thought I would save Glynne the bother of having to park up and look for me loitering at the main entrance like a spare part. My plan was that as he drove in, I could flag him down, he could pick me up by my car in the car park and we would be off to the game prompt-ish. But I missed him, he parked up and was waiting at the main entrance wondering where I was. A somewhat terse text asked where I might be. Damn it. I tried to help but only succeeded in making matters worse. I quickly checked that I had all my stuff and had to trot with my rucksack and physio bag back to the main entrance where I should have been in the first place. So much for cutting him off at the pass. I was knackered and I hadn't got any further than the main entrance to the building. Rhys was to be the physio for the final. I figured, rather naively as it turned out, that I had the evening off but the mega-bag travelled with me just in case. We had a final to get to and I had messed Glynne about, so no more time to waste.

As I got into the back of Glynne's car I was greeted by two other moiderers, Les money and Rob. They had too many e-numbers during the day, or something more recreational, as all three were talking ten to the dozen. Less so the manic 'Marvel' superheroes but more *Dad's Army*. I jumped in with the *Dad's Army* platoon and we zoomed off with a plan to beat the Boche. Well Boded really. Glynne fitted the bill as the pompous and ineffectual Captain Mainwaring, Les money as the blustering Jonesy telling us not to panic when Les was panicking and Rob was Frazer with a beady eye pinning you back whilst Rob delivered salvos of foreboding stories of doom. I guess I fitted the bill of Pikey, forever incapable of looking after myself. Les promptly launched into the quality of the refereeing this season and how it could have been improved with even the slightest passing interest by referees in the FAW rules. Les money at this point wasn't panicking.

After what seemed to be hours of crossing a tree deprived rocky tundra which resembled a lunar landscape that was in reality the far end of Anglesey, admittedly a bit greener than what I suspect the moon looks like; we started off amongst more minor roads that the platoon knew pretty intimately. So far so good. Then an argument broke out as to which was the best route to take. By now Les was showing signs of stress and Rob thought that we would never get there. Well one eye of Rob's did. Fortunately, the huge otherworldly structure of Wylfa came to our rescue as it popped into view somewhat unexpectedly, and then we knew we must be close to Cemaes Bay. The road meandered past the sleeping nuclear giant but Cemaes temporarily escaped our gaze, presumably hiding in a moon crater or behind a further turn in the road.

Phews all around, as we were greeted with the 'Welcome to Cemaes Bay' road sign. It was not followed by 'twinned with eternal glory for 1876' but it should have been. We could not be far away now, surely? Jonesy said that we should turn left at the roundabout in town. He began to panic in the Jonesy jittery way as he remembered that he previously approached Cemaes Bay from the opposite direction.

Fortunately, with the instinctive reflexes expected of a home guard captain, Glynne took a right and we were once again making progress. Jonesy and Frazer were silenced. We then missed the football ground ignoring the huge throngs of perhaps three or four people crossing the street in front of the car to what was obviously the venue and we were soon heading out of town and deep into nowhere. We had made a committee decision and, like any committee worth its salt, we took too long and made the wrong choice. To add to our plight, the AA hadn't seen fit to advise the huge volumes of football traffic of the available parking arrangements for at least half a dozen cars to park in the surrounding streets. We passed a sleepy dog by the roadside who took a little interest in the lost car that had strayed out of Cemaes Bay and the strange arguing occupants but then the dog laid its head down and appeared to go back to sleep. We passed some goats who looked up to investigate the minor commotion in the lane next to their field but then looked at each other and returned to chewing their grass. Once again, we were in the depths of the unforgiving Anglesey moonscape. An executive decision was made, Mainwaring managed a swift U-turn and headed back into town before grinding to a halt the wrong way in the town's only one-way street. The Eagle had landed. Well the boys from Walmington-on-Sea had. And we were still 15 minutes' walk away from the ground itself. When we got to what felt like Wembley Way we were surprised to find that there were ample parking spaces all around. Oh well, we all needed some exercise after such a long drive but I brought some huge sausage rolls for us to gobble later on, in an attempt to save the situation. I must admit I drove to Bodedern in the winter, which is also at the far end of Anglesey for us mainlanders, without the incessant moidering from *Dad's Army* but using my car's satnav instead, and got there without incident.

I imagine the four of us walking out of a smoke-filled backdrop of flares going off in slow motion as we entered the stadium of destiny just, well slightly, like a scene from the film *Armageddon* as the heroes are about to rocket off to save the world from a grim meteorite. Obviously, I would be the Ben Affleck character. The other three would remain as the *Dad's Army* disaster merchants that would inevitably send us to our doom.

As it happened, I was not so heroic as I left my money in my car back at the hospital so the Captain had to pay my entrance fee. Yet again. I owed too many beers by now so I hoped that Glynne would forget about my debt to society. Well to him at least.

"Stupid boy!" uttered Glynne, unintentionally aping the bumbling Army Captain. I must admit this was a comment with some justification.

Oh, and there was a football game to see. The pitch was perfectly manicured, with stripes. I think turf is in great shape if it has stripes. I guess that gives the game away that I am not a gardener but I do like my garden just so. The evening weather was perfect to view and play football: sunny, warm but not hot and just a gentle breeze. Just like that game earlier in the season at Llanberis. There were one or two wispy clouds that didn't appear to have any desire to give us a good soaking. The late spring sun was slowly setting over the undulating hills of Anglesey. The sort of picture to paint dreamy memories of possible glory. A capacity crowd of 500 or so spectators were in fine voice to add to the sense of occasion. There were three sheds for the spectators to protect them from sunburn but there were no Twin Towers of Wembley and no Wembley Arch.

Alas, to put you out of your misery, the game was won in the first minute with perhaps simply an innocent foul in chopping Logs, Boded's best player and, all too often, a lethal centre forward. Logs spent the next five minutes limping around the place until he had to be substituted. Cynical, surely not, not even a booking but I think Dyl Bach knew Logs must not get the better of him or of any of our defence.

Both teams' benches were constantly shouting instructions to their respective players as well as to the ref for various perceived dodgy decisions. Most vocal was Merv. He didn't seem to draw breath between issuing missives to Ben the goalie and to our defence.

"Don't let him get his head up," he repeatedly screamed.

I tried to work out what that meant as all players had their heads up to avoid smashing into each other any more often than they normally end up doing. After several minutes of watching and listening to Merv I had to ask.

"What do you mean by don't let him get his head up Merv?"

He looked at me as if in pain to have to explain the bleeding obvious.

"If you let the f-ing defender raise his head he can see where to pass the f-ing ball." To paraphrase somewhat.

I wondered how you stop someone raising their head but I decided that one question was all that I was allowed. I must attend more training sessions.

He also had a touching chat to a small boy behind him on the other side of the rails to explain how important it was that the goalie should not rush to distribute the ball if we were winning. Merv has a heart of gold. Just don't tell him.

Labrador Chris again noted his vaping friend in the adjacent dugout. Chris didn't say anything this time. We had the measure of Boded. The Jackson Five didn't show either.

Les (darker top) muscling his way around Boded. Cam Barry and Dyl Bach in the background. Picture courtesy of Dafydd Hughes.

After 30 minutes a goalmouth scramble ensued in the Boded penalty area when their goalie fumbled the ball, Les the Truck managed to head the ball across goal for none other than the towering Tom Clark to head in at point blank range. Tom was to get married two days later and vowed to stay away. He missed the Pwllheli game earlier in the week, but vows are just words. Tom couldn't miss the final. He came to the real party to gain eternal glory for 1876. Five minutes later and a Boded own goal made it 2-0 and that was the way it stayed to half time.

In the second half, we were then in game management mode in keeping Boded at arm's length from our goal with Ben having to make only two saves all game. To add to Boded's woes Les, who with several of our lot, was having a fine evening, placed a superb measured pass to the charging Corrig who in turn, chipped the Boded goalie from 30 yards to send the ball arcing like a shooting star into the Boded net to make it 3-0 at full time. The League Cup was ours, well a small shield, but who cares as we had won and now we had silverware to adorn the trophy cabinet of our trophy room, for which we needed a trophy cabinet and a trophy room. Winning cups appear to have hidden costs.

Dave Jones from his Grassroots North Wales website concluded: "Bangor 1876... won their first-ever knockout competition when they picked up the Premier Division Cup at Cemaes Bay on Thursday, courtesy of goals from Tom Clarke, Corrig McGonigle and an own goal".

Injuries were a plenty and all seemed to be at the opposite end of the pitch to which I was standing at the time of each injury: with a nose bleed, a head injury, a tweaked ankle, lots of cramp and the inevitable injury to Gethin. I had a quick chat with Geth just before the start.
"Whatever you do, look after yourself, I am fed up of patching you up."
"I'll do my best Doc."

Ten minutes later he had a pulled hamstring. Bless him, young Geth looked at me apologetically. Les also squished a Boded player in the second half. Les, being a truck, shall we say is a bit of a unit, and rendered a Boded player acutely two dimensional. That needed some attention from the Boded staff until his third dimension returned and thankfully was able to continue. Rhys and I were exhausted by full time. We dined out on those huge sausage rolls hiding in my rucksack that my *Dad's Army* friends didn't get round to munch.

Important seeming people gave out trophies to the match officials. We even had a fourth official for the game, who stood between the team dugouts and attended seemingly only to receive verbal abuse from both sets of managerial staff directly in his ears for the entire duration of the game. He was entirely powerless to do anything about any of the multitude of complaints. It must have been an important game to have proper linesmen and a fourth official. There was a lukewarm response from the Bangor faithful for all the men in black. Almost all the Boded supporters had left or were not up for making much noise. Medals were handed to the losing team. Again, at best, a modest response generated mostly from the Bangor faithful. Medals and the shield were then handed to our lads. The Boded team were gracious in defeat and applauded 1876. Les raised the shield and the place erupted with singing, cheers, fireworks and the obligatory blue flares. Bliss.

Returning home with the *Dad's Army* was incident free. Perhaps this was a bit of a surprise but the four of us were replete with cup success as the Captain pointed his car in the general direction of the Welsh mainland and the huge Snowdonia mountain range looming over the island with the mountains still clearly visible even in the late spring moonlight. I gave Les money a Blue Riband chocolate biscuit he demands from me for every game. Best to keep on the sweet side of a former bank manager. He was happy. Soon we were on the A55 and heading back to Bangor.

Les raises the standard for 1876. Picture courtesy of Dafydd Hughes.

Delayed decision of our team's fate

The Intermediate Challenge Cup semi-final, two days after the glorious League Cup final success, was yet again against Boded but was cancelled by the Bodedern team. The official reason given to the North Wales Coast FA was that they had too few fit players to field a team. To make matters worse, Boded had a few players who received injuries playing us in the preceding game. Were they spooked by the two recent defeats at our hands? Their forward, Logs was rooted to the physio couch. As a consequence of this cancellation, we were given a bye to the final against Rhyl, which was originally scheduled for 31st May, but was delayed due to lack of availability of a suitable venue to host the final. The talk was that this was to be played during pre-season later in the summer.

No matter, our next priority is to strengthen the first team squad for next season. When I spoke to Johno after the end of the season, he felt that there were no concerns of players being grabbed by bigger clubs and he said that he had no players that wished to leave. There may be better prospects to entice new players to Bangor 1876 if we progressed to the Ardal league following our runners-up position in the league at the end of the season.

Our wishes were to be answered by the genie from the lamp of footballing fortune which we had been rubbing since the Boded league game in early May. On 9th June, the FAW announced at a meeting of their National Leagues Board that the FAW had accepted an application from Bangor 1876 to be promoted to tier three, the Ardal League North West; this would mean that for the first time we would have the opportunity to compete in a national league, from the start of following season. They didn't say whether or not it was because of the excellent service provided by Rhys, Trudy and me but I'm sure it was.

From now on, we will have to travel further afield for our away games, curiously as far as the English border despite being in a western Welsh league. We will have to pay more for match officials as we will have two linesmen to visit us to add to the ref's fee instead of each team each supplying a potentially biased linesman. Recalling the Llanberis goal that never was on that sunny afternoon, the next time Corrig wafts an angelic lob over the oppo goalie then maybe it will not be ruled out as offside.

And, somehow destiny makes its mark, as amongst others, we will be playing against Boded again.
"001876 we meet again."
C'MON BANGOR!

The story continues…

The glory boys. From left to right: Cully, Cam Barry, Shaun Lock, Cian Williams, Cian Thomas (dark tracksuit top at the back), Tom Clarke, Ben Owen (dark tracksuit top kneeling), Mark Hawkins (dark tracksuit top at the back), Dyl Bach, Asser (kneeling), Corey Jones, Steelo (kneeling), Geth, Les with shield, Sion Eds (and not Sioned: dark tracksuit top), Corrig, H and Ben (last four kneeling). Mad crazy fans also in on the act. Picture courtesy of Dafydd Hughes.

Epilogue

Dafydd had done his sums for the season's activities. He had calculated that our centre forwards, Corrig and Les scored 70 goals in league and cup games between them with Corrig just getting to polish the golden boot by a narrow margin despite joining the club midway through our season. Unlike Corrig, Les was with 1876 all of the current campaign. An incredible total of 176 goals was scored in league and cup by Bangor 1876 which even surpasses the efforts of Manchester City who were the top free-scoring European side in the same season tucking away a mere 150 goals. Say no more. I was pleased with my three assists for the season inasmuch as I strapped Les' ankle which led to three goals from the mighty Truck. He did thank me when I pressed home this point. Stretching the definition of assisting goals I admit, but I feel I am Bangor's answer to Kevin de Bruyne. I'll see if I can improve my stats and perhaps my miserable footballing skills for the following campaign.

At an end of season award ceremony held at Tafarn Y Glôb (the Globe pub), a favourite local hostelry in Upper Bangor, the unflappable Tom Clarke was awarded the Fans' Player of the Year and I can confirm that he did successfully become a married man without injury. So he said. Cully led the defence with flawless performances week after week and was awarded Players' Player of the Year. Ben Heald, who retired at the end of the season, was presented with a special achievement award. At one point in the season old man Ben managed to keep a clean sheet for 440 minutes of playing time. He spent an entire season barking orders out to the team that could be heard across Treborth whether Bangor was playing there or anywhere else across North Wales.

Ben, our senior goalie, giving the ball the eye. A rare sight as the action was usually at the other end. We'll miss you Ben. Picture courtesy of Dafydd Hughes

From a medical point of view, we had three head injuries (two at the same time), one broken ankle and a broken wrist as well as a host of soft tissue injuries which I managed to fumble my way through.

Rhys and I said our summer time good-byes to Johno and Mel after the final. Johno was still smiling like a Cheshire cat. Mel was pleased with our efforts and he likened the close teamwork between Rhys and me to the Two Ronnies. Then a dispute followed as to who was Barker and who was Corbett. Other inspirational partnerships could have been considered such as the pioneers of powered flight, the Wright brothers or the musical virtuosos, Simon and Garfunkel or more likely the Chuckle Brothers.

As Ronnie Barker once announced "And now a sketch featuring Ronnie Corbett whose wife thinks he's the salt of the earth. That's why she keeps him in the cellar". Perhaps that is where I should be kept for the general safety of all at 1876. Well with Trudy returning for the following season we would be the three musketeers being all for one and one for all!

On a reflective note, there is a palpable connection with the local community throughout the club. We have had a difficult time since our start in life. Sport, as in many walks of life, had been turned upside down because of the pandemic. By the end of the current season, Bangor 1876 had been in business for three years and had not yet experienced a complete schedule of matches throughout any single year, with one season entirely chalked off and the other two with games cancelled and many rescheduled. The expectation is that full programmes of matches will be available going forward.

There is a deep-seated pride shining throughout the team. When all is said and done, they are a respectful and pleasant group of lads. Don't get me wrong, during a game they are forthright and vocal and physically are combat ready, but off the pitch they are considerate young people personally I am proud to know. Saying they are like the few who saved Blighty during the Battle of Britain may be a bit strong though I would dare to suggest they are of a similar mentality giving all for each other, expecting the same back and not asking for anything except victory. I know that the *Dad's Army* platoon and the rest of the moiderers are proud of them. The wider club all know each other and all the fans are able to regularly meet the team. Small children, in particular, idolise them. I felt enormously privileged to see the commitment from the first team, the training staff, my physio colleagues, the directors, the sales, kitchen and ticket staff. To state the obvious, 1876 would be nothing if it wasn't for the support of the wider community and the regular attendance of our 400 or so dedicated fans who lift the place for every game. Blue flares and all.

Johno, in an interview with Jonathan Ervine at the season's end talking of his first few months as first team manager said: "I knew what a fantastic job Mel and Dyl [the previous first team manager] had done so it was always going to be tough to continue or improve on that". He added: "a special mention has to go to coaches Mel, Gaz, Aled, Merv and Chris who have supported every decision along the way and are always there to offer advice and guidance".

We three musketeers even got a mention! "Also, the medical staff, nothing is ever too much for them. They always make sure at least one is available for training and games and are willing to pull together when needed."

The Chairman, Glynne Roberts had something to say about our direction of travel. "In looking forward, we hope to foster closer links with the Women's teams, and to develop our junior section. As a fan owned club, we are also keen to foster closer links with the local community, and hope to develop a programme over the next season to enhance those links. To achieve our ambitions, we need everyone on board." He added: "Bangor 1876 is about all of us working together".

John Dexter Jones was circumspect. "The promotion has attracted ire from Caernarfon and Boded. We are now in the same league as Rhyl which is the biggest team in the Welsh League. Ardal means we now have a referee but also two official linesmen, not surrogates from the two opposing teams, a proper fixture list, and better quality away pitches. This will be a tough league."

So, no VAR or PA announcements at our games just yet. Oh well, I will have to be patient. We are planning to get a scoreboard to tell us the score before our phone Apps confirm what we suspected later in the day. That is progress. I hope it will be a scoreboard that always tells us we are winning. Our new local derby in the Ardal League will be with Y Felinheli and although it is a little further afield than our previous local derby with Menai Bridge Tigers, a record breaking 40 yards away, John hoped that it could draw a big crowd.

John added: "Ardal league clubs have more supporters. It may be better that we do not get promoted too quickly to manage our finances and improve facilities. We can then get better sponsorship, get better players".

Pete Jones expects the next season to be a difficult one. "We hope for better grounds and officials and we hope to strengthen our squad with new signings."

I did a quick straw poll from a random selection of the 1876 ne'er-do-wells about their ambitions for the coming season. Our esteemed directors advised that the first team facilities needed to be improved to be compliant with the FAW regulations for tier two. We may possibly need a new ground. Their various responses expressed ambition for the team to gain promotion as quickly as possible. At the very least, they collectively wished for all to enjoy the football and for 1876 to be competitive in the Ardal League. After all, there are some big teams to provide serious tests of our season-long ability. Armed with this advice, the picture appeared clear, and then I spoke to Mel, the first team manager, who without drawing breath announced "well, just to win the bloody thing". Fantastic.

In fairness, he added a few other bits to his glorious wish list, with an ambition to see squad improvement and providing competition for team places, to improve our junior set-up with prospects for juniors to be able to progress to the first team, to increase ground seating to 250 places and finally, if we progress to tier two, we would be permitted to develop a junior academy which was Mel's previous role at Bangor City and currently he is devoting more of his time to junior training. An academy will be beneficial for us as it will attract more coaches as well as high quality juniors which can be retained in the club. So I'm with you Mel!

Aled managed to reach the summit of Kilimanjaro despite feeling the effects of walking at high altitude. He has raised more than £3,000 for his chosen mental health charity, Mind. In his typically modest way, Kilimanjaro is over and he quickly returned to training the squad.

Medical expenses for the club have been minimal to date. Rhys and I required an FAW first aider update course, both attracting a small fee. Trudy had hers already. There is a constant requirement to buy tapes, bandages, sprays and creams. These were addressed speedily, of course, by Dafydd. We ordered physio bags and a stretcher. We may need a chest freezer to store ice for the ice bath. I have displayed infinite generosity as I bought various analgesics, salt tablets, oranges, blister plasters and some tampons. I have checked that the tampons I bought for nose bleeds are small enough to fit into my nose assuming my nostrils are an average size. More importantly I managed to get them out again.

The FAW requires additional medical equipment for tier two: an oxygen cylinder and mask as well as a blood pressure monitor would be needed. Hopefully these will be inexpensive additions to our medical supplies. Although medical cover to date has not been a big resource this season, I think this would become more expensive in subsequent seasons in higher leagues if further promotions come our way. Tier one requires each player to have a medical examination including a few heart tests. I dream of an all-terrain medical buggy which I have seen used in rugby international games. That is the white one with a flashing light on a pole with the small wheels which looks so cool but sadly remains beyond the empty pockets of Les money.

I need to consider the development of the role of the club doctor which includes my future with Bangor 1876. There is a clear ambition for the club to progress to tier two or even the Welsh Premier League and perhaps, by then, a team doctor with expertise in sport science may be preferred. On a personal note I need to keep my professional medical registration and professional indemnity (a form of insurance) paid and my ability to keep my medical practice up-to-date. That is not so easy after retirement. Yet the paradox is that after retirement I have the time to commit to the cause. On balance, I guess that means I would be likely to step down after two to three seasons but remain a moiderer and fan wherever my family ties may take me. By then I hope that I will be able to look back with pride to think that I have had a small role in the progress of an amazing community project and footballing feelgood story that is Bangor 1876.

133

I have learnt a lot about sports medicine, though I admit I have a lot more to learn, but even more about humanity and what it is to have a belonging to a community with a common goal. Or 176 goals! Give us more of the same boys!

In the end the greater game has been won already. We are a community to represent Bangor in all that is good about the city in being there for each other and supporting all when the chips are down. With our early success we bring bigger challenges. We will not win every game and sometimes we will be on the receiving end of heavy defeats. There is much to take from the manner of any defeat and we go again, tougher, stronger and with more ambition. We are a family club managed by our supporters. Mutual support and benefit are all important. This is relevant also to all our fellow teams who deal with the same issues and gain a similar camaraderie in supporting each and all.

There is an entire spectrum of people who give their time willingly, and often freely, just to help and to enjoy a communion that appears greater than the sum of its parts. I suspect the same is true for many of your local sportsmen who give up their spare time just for the sheer pleasure of competing. If you are not already involved then just get stuck in, whether directly in whatever activity takes your fancy or in a supportive role. Like me, you just may be pleasantly surprised.

I still haven't managed to get a key to the stockroom cupboard yet, though I have found the stretcher and the massage couch. The University has bought a bright red wheelie bin to go into the shower of our changing room to be the ice bath. It is sitting in an office just now and we are trying to stop plonkers throwing their rubbish into it despite a large notice on the front saying that it is not to be used as a waste bin.

There is a significant postscript to this story, in that the Intermediate Challenge Cup final against Rhyl was cancelled at the outset of the following season due to difficulty in finding a suitable date for the clash. The date offered on the August Bank Holiday was at a time that 1876 were unable to field a team. This was sad, but CPD Y Rhyl 1879 FC found itself in the same Ardal League for the subsequent season as our newly promoted 1876, and so both may compete for promotion to tier two. All exciting stuff.

At the first game of the following season, Cabs, the ticket guy, called me Simon. Result.

A beautiful vista: the beautiful game. Picture courtesy of Matt Johnson.

Perhaps the last words should come from our great leader Johno. I asked him how he could hold on to the respect of the dressing room when there has been a series of defeats.

"I dunno mate, it hasn't happened yet!"

Bangor 1876 honours

North Wales Coast West Football League Division One champions	2020
Supporters Direct Europe best limerick	2020
North Wales Coast West Football League Premier Division runners up	2022
League Cup winners	2022
Les Pegler's discounted parking ticket	2022

The team
Sam Ashworth, Cam Barry, Tom Clarke, Joe (Cully) Culshaw, Les Davies, Sion (Sion Eds) Edwards, Harry (H) Galleotti, Mark Hawkins, Aaron (Asser) Heald, Ben (Asser's Dad) Heald, Corey Jones, Shaun Lock, Corrig McGonigle, Ben Owen, Jamie (Pets) Petrie, Alwyn Roberts, Sam Roberts, Luke (Steelo) Steele, Cian Thomas, Gethin (Geth) Thomas, Cian Williams, Dylan (Dyl Bach) Williams.

The team managers and coaching staff
Aled Hughes, Michael (Johno) Johnston, Chris Jones, Mel Jones, Gareth (Gaz) Williams, Mervyn Williams.

The wider team
James Deakin, John Dexter-Jones, Jonathan Ervine, Dylan Fernley, Frida Fernley, Dafydd Hughes, Matt Johnson, Llion Jones, Peter Jones, Rob Lewis, Les Pegler, Glynne Roberts, Linda Roberts, Rich Williams, Robin Williams.

My mentors
I have reserved until last the two most important and supportive colleagues in the club who have taught me all I know on a steep learning curve about soft tissue injuries. Thank you so much Rhys Last and Trudy Owen. Trudy I am sorry you had to miss the latter half of the season. It was good to have you back later in the summer.

I am sorry if I have unintentionally offended anyone in putting my experiences and thoughts to paper. To the rest, man-up.

Acknowledgements

To my wife Linda, for involuntarily becoming a literary widow having me disappear to the study for hours on end, to Alan, my father-in-law and lifelong Toffee, to Luke, my son-in-law and his father Jerry who have had to suffer various drafts of the manuscript. Thank you, Glynne (the boss - although parallels with Springsteen end there) for your kind multiple reviews of the manuscript and as always, a rich source of priceless gossip. Rob Lewis, your forensic review of the manuscript nearly killed me but left me stronger. I thank you for your immense generosity of time and effort. Jamie Petrie provided funding for my 'project' without question to enable me to publish. That is kindness indeed. Michael Johnston with his patience, wit and honest opinions of life in charge. Gratitude bro. Dafydd Hughes and Matt Johnson who have been so generous with the use of their pictures amongst other things. To our opponents and colleagues on the pitch, of course including Boded, who have all been such good sports.

Most of all to the fans who turn up in rain or shine to watch the lads do their utmost, to moider and have a great time. You are special.

Bibliography

1. afefootballnews
   https://afefootballnews.com/2020/05/25/gwynedd
   -league-2019-20-bangorstorm-to-title-in-first-
   season-as-a-club/
2. Bangor 1876 – Business plan 2022-2025. April
   2022
3. Bangor 1876 https://www.bangor1876.com
4. Bangor 1876 9-0 CPD Pentraeth: Citizens on
   Cloud Nine in opening day win
   https://clwbpeldroed.org/2021/07/03/bangor-1876-
   cpd-pentraeth-match-updates/
5. Bangor Comrades 25.05.2022
   http://www.johndexterjones.com
6. BBC News 01.12.2021
   https://www.bbc.co.uk/sport/football/59096474
7. BBC Sport 16.07.2012
   https://www.bbc.co.uk/sport/football/18864565
8. Bêl yn y Gogledd
   https://belynygogledd.wordpress.com/2021/05/05/
   lionel-messi-to-les-davies-a-throwback-to-the-
   2011-12-uefa-best-player-in-europe-award/
9. Daily Post 12.07.2019
   https://www.dailypost.co.uk/sport/football/football
   -news/bangor-1876-take-field-first-16622114
10. Farewell to Farrar Road. 50 key events that shaped
    the history of Bangor City. Bangor City Supporters
    Association. Glynne Roberts
11. FAW Tier 2 Club Licencing Regulations 2021
    https://www.faw.cymru/files/6416/3118/4108/FA
    W_Tier_2_Club_Licensing_Regulations_2021.pdf
12. Football Association of Wales
    https://www.faw.cymru
13. Football Association of Wales

https://www.faw.cymru/en/news/ambitious-plan-develop-referees/

14. Four Seasons. A Bangor Football Concerto. Lightning Source UK Ltd. John Dexter Jones.

15. Grassroots North Wales Chwaraeon Y Gogs https://nwsport.co.uk/2019/12/15/gwynedd-league-bangor-1876-hit-100-goals-nefyn-go-nap-six-for-beganifs-plus-updated-stats-for-1876/

16. Grassroots North Wales Chwaraeon Y Gogs https://nwsport.co.uk/2019/12/22/bangor-1876-attract-better-crowds-than-rangers-or-liverpool/

17. Grassroots North Wales Chwaraeon Y Gogs 27.05.22 https://nwsport.co.uk

18. https://belynygogledd.wordpress.com/ accessed 30.05.2022

19. John Dexter Jones http://www.johndexterjones.com/a-paradise-regained/

20. John Dexter Jones http://www.johndexterjones.com/fcum-away/

21. Mirror 17.07.2012 https://www.mirror.co.uk/sport/football/news/bangor-citys-les-davies-nominated-1146215

22. Poem of Quotes https://www.poemofquotes.com accessed 30.04.22

23. Sportskeeda https://www.sportskeeda.com/

24. The Bangor Aye 18.09.2017 https://www.thebangoraye.com/essential-bangor-words-every-student-should-know/

25. The Bangor Aye 01.10.2021 https://www.thebangoraye.com

26. The Bangor Aye 15.11.2021 https://www.thebangoraye.com/bangor-comrades-announce-new-abbey-road-album/

27. The Banger Aye 30.04.22 https://www.thebangoraye.com/bodedern-

crowned-champions-after-bangor-1876-fall-at-glantraeth/ BBC News 12.09.2021 https://www.bbc.co.uk

28. The football collective. Academic voice of football 02.08.2020 https://football-collective.co.uk/2020/08/02/bangor-1876-a-fan-owned-team-with-a-link-to-the-2018- football-collective-conference/

29. The Guardian https://www.theguardian.com/uk/2004/aug/07/arts news.wales

30. The North Wales Chronicle 01.12.2021 https://www.northwaleschronicle.co.uk/news/1975 4750.bangor-comrades-announce-abbey-road-album-support-community-centre/

31. the Referees' Association https://www.the-ra.org/

32. Y Clwb Pêl-Droed The football club https://clwbpeldroed.org/2022/02/23/bangor- 1876-corrig-mcgonigle-conwy-borough/

The Author

In my spare time, I enjoy walking and real ale. I was an exceptionally direct yet ungifted downhill skier in years gone by and could deal with any piste as long as all the moguls were aligned in the right places. I am a life-long supporter of Manchester City Football Club though a hopeless footballer. I run slowly for long distances. I have completed the London marathon once and the Great North Run four times. I have attended occasional Grands Prix which involved standing for long periods of time in mud to watch very fast cars break down.

I have two fabulously expensive daughters who have grown up and are now hurling their expenses at their partners, and not their parents. I am learning to cook rather late in life; my wife accepts that I may destroy most of our pots and pans.

Milton Keynes UK
Ingram Content Group UK Ltd.
UKHW020626151123
432605UK00010B/272

Printed in Great Britain
by Amazon

49441049R00067